FINGERPRINT

FINGERPRINT

THE ART OF USING HANDMADE ELEMENTS IN GRAPHIC DESIGN

BY CHEN DESIGN ASSOCIATES

WITH FOREWORD
BY MICHAEL MABRY

AND ESSAYS FROM
ROSS MACDONALD
DEBBIE MILLMAN
JEAN ORLEBEKE
JIM SHERRADEN
MARTIN VENEZKY

HOW
BOOKS
Cincinnati, Ohio
www.howdesign.com

IF YOU STARTED your GRAPHIC DESIGN CAREER bEFORE THE mid 1980s, as I DID, YOU CREATED all YOUR ART by HAND. ALL YOUR iDEAS WERE SKETCHED OUT, THEN CRAFTED BY HAND AND PRESENTED DELICATELY TO THE CLIENT. YOU LEARNED to SPEC TYPE ON TYPE-written MANUSCRIPTS, WHITE OUT AND ALL, WHICH the TYPOGRAPHERS WOULD THEN deciPHER. TYPE SET GALLEYS WOULD RETURN in A DAY OR TWO COMPOSED AND PROOFREAD, READY TO BE CUT and PASTED ON TO A RULED OUT BOARD TO YOUR SPECIFICATIONS. The FINAL ART WAS called MECHANICAL ART, A SERIES of ART BOARDS WITH TYPE AND fPOs PASTED INTO POSITION WITH ALL THE INFORMATION AbOUT the JOB THAT WAS PRINTING. many DESIGNERS TOOK GREAT PRIDE iN CREATING IMPECCABLE MECHANICALS, REINFORCING THE IMPORTANCE of CRAFT IN OUR PROFESSION—THE BELIEF that IF YOU TOOK GREAT CARE PREPARING YOUR MECHANICALS, THE PRE-PRESS PERSON WORKING ON IT WOULD PUT THAT SAME CARE INTO YOUR PROJECT. CRAFTSMEN working TOGETHER TO CREATE A PIECE Of PURPOSEFUL ART WAS a GRATIFYING MIX of INTELLECTUAL and PHYSICAL CHALLENGES. WHEN THE COMPUTER CAME ON THE GRAPHIC DESIGN SCENE IN THE MID-1980s, I WAS VERY EXCITED to LEARN HOW TO CREATE ON IT. MY ENTHUSIASM WANED QUICKLY WHEN I REALIZED we WERE in THE MIDDLE Of A VERY expensive LAB EXPERIMENT. The COMPUTERS of THAT TIME HAD small MONITOR SCREENS AND MOVED VERY SLOWLY. I VIVIDLY REMEMBER MAKING a SMALL MOVE ON A file AND the COMPUTER bEGINNING TO CHURN. I WOULD THEN LEAVE MY OFFICE, WALK DOWN SIX FLIGHTS of STAIRS, CROSS THE STREET AND GET A CUP of COFFEE, WALK BACK TO MY BUILDING, RIDE THE ELEVATOR UP TO THE SIXTH FLOOR and RETURN TO MY DESK ASTONISHED THAT THE COMPUTER WAS STILL CHURNING to COMPLETE THE COMMAND. THE INTENSE FOCUS ON TECHNOLOGY STARTED TO CLOUD MY CREATIVE JUDGMENT. I FOUND myself FINDING WAYS TO WORK WITH THE COMPUTER'S CAPAbILITIES RATHER THAN WITH MY OWN. FOR EXAMPLE I WOULD RELY ON THE SIMPLEST

detail
Summer Cover
The Land of Nod
2005

detail
Antidote Press
Limited Edition Print
2006

PATH of LEAST RESISTANCE IF I HAD A TIGHT DEADLINE. I WOULD CREATE IMAGES AS VECTOR files BECAUSE IT WAS EASIER for THE COMPUTER TO MANAGE VERSUS GETTING BOGGED DOWN WITH HIGH RESOLUTION FILES. This APPROACH DID NOT SIT WELL WITH ME AND I BECAME CREATIVELY RESTLESS. AFTER WORKING THIRTEEN YEARS IN THE BUSINESS, I NEEDED to STEP AWAY AND EVALUATE WHAT I WAS DOING.

ON THE WEEKENDS, I STARTED MAKING PRIMITIVE WOOD TOYS. I WOULD CUT SIMPLE SHAPES OUT of SCRAP WOOD AND GLUE SNIPS OF UTILITARIAN ADVERTISING FROM Popular Science AND Science and Mechanics MAGAZINES. Then I WOULD COVER THE FORM WITH SHELLAC, LET IT DRY, BUFF IT OUT with STEEL WOOL AND REPEAT THE PROCESS AGAIN UNTIL THE SURFACE WAS SMOOTH. THEN I WOULD PAINT LETTER FORMS, NUMBERS AND STRIPES OVER THE SURFACE. There WAS NO OBVIOUS REASON WHY I WAS MAKING these TOYS, ALTHOUGH IT WAS a WELCOME BREAK FROM THE COMPUTER. SOON I WAS INCORPORATING THIS GARAGE-BUILT METHOD in SOME OF MY PROJECTS. I WAS CREATING IMAGES BY GLUING PRINTED EPHEMERA ON PLANKS OF WOOD SEALED with SHELLAC AND THEN CAPTURING IT DIGITALLY BY the FLATBED SCANNER. I WAS USING MY HANDS AGAIN, WHICH WAS REALLY LIBERATING.

DURING THIS TIME MY WIFE AND I WERE in THE PROCESS OF MAKING SOME BIG LIFE CHANGES. WE ADOPTED a CHILD FROM THE PEOPLE'S REPUBLIC of CHINA. BECOMING A FIRST TIME PARENT IS A TOTAL MIND-BENDING EXPERIENCE. SLEEP DEPRIVATION ASIDE, I STRUGGLED, AS MANY NEW PARENTS DO, with BALANCING WORK dEADLINES, HOME RESPONSIBILITIES, AS WELL AS ADAPTING TO new PRIMAL SCREAMS IN IN THE HOUSE. This IS ALL PRETTY NORMAL STUFF. WHAT I DID NOT EXPECT WAS PONDERING MY LEGACY. HOW DID I WANT MY DAUGHTER to REMEMBER ME? I DEFINITELY WANTED HER TO REMEMBER ME AS A GOOD father, BUT ALSO AS A GRAPHIC DESIGNER. THE THOUGHT of LEAVING HER a COPY OF A CORPORATE BROCHURE I HAD DESIGNED DIDN'T SEEM QUITE RIGHT. I WANTED TO LEAVE HER SOMETHING I HAD MADE WITH MY OWN HANDS, SOMETHING THAT EVOKED MY PRESENCE WHEN SHE looked AT IT OR TOUCHED IT. SOMETHING THAT CAME FROM THE HEART. SO I PICKED UP WHERE I LEFT OFF IN THE GARAGE, although I WAS GLUING AND PAINTING ON CARDBOARD RATHER THAN WOOD, PAINTING WITH GOUACHE RATHER THAN enamel HOUSE PAINT.

To CREATE AN IMAGE THAT REVEALS SOMETHING ABOUT the ARTIST AS WELL AS ENGAGES THE VIEWER TAKES SKILL. YOU JUST DON'T SIT DOWN AND BANG OUT SOMETHING THAT EMBODIES MULTIPLE EMOTIONS ON THE first TRY. THIS IS A LIFE-LONG PURSUIT. I KNEW I HAD MY WORK CUT OUT FOR ME. I HAD TO GET STARTED.

THIS IS MY STORY. NOW TAKE a LOOK AT THE DESIGNERS and ARTISTS SHOWCASED IN THIS BOOK. THEY SHARE THEIR STORIES AS WELL. WHAT'S YOURS?

Audition
Adobe Systems, Inc.
2006

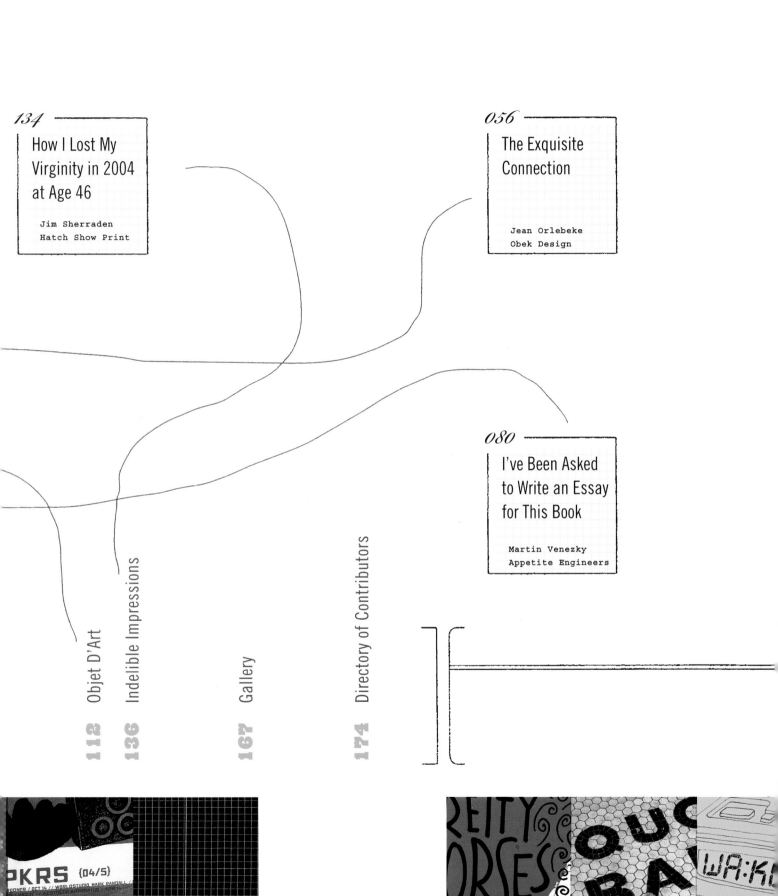

01

LETTERING

Letterforms created by hand
(complete with irregular weights and personal foibles)
communicate directly to the reader on a human level,
making the message that much more accessible.

Kelham MacLean wine labels

Comment: The Kelham MacLean winery is a partnership between a high-end grape grower and a renowned Napa Valley winemaker. Rather than develop a logo for the winery, we treated the name like a signature to speak to this partnership. Kelham MacLean produces high-end, handcrafted wines, and they wanted their labels to reflect this level of quality. We used classic turn-of-the-century French typography, printed a faded edge, letterpressed the type and laser cut rounded corners and a perforation to give the bottles an air of sophistication.

Design: Templin Brink Design **Art Directors:** Gaby Brink, Joel Templin **Designer:** Gaby Brink **Client:** Kelham MacLean Wines **Materials:** offset printed, letterpress printed, pin perfed

Delaware Sessions CD packaging

Design: Smackbottom, Inc. **Art Director:**
Leif Fairfield **Designer:** Alice Koswara **Client:**
Leif Fairfield **Materials:** illustration, letterpress
Printer: Leif Fairfield, One Heart Press

Comment: Since CDs can be purchased for about ten cents per dozen, musician Leif
Fairfield wanted to create an object that would be cherished more than simply another
CD. We decided to create a hand illustration that could be printed letterpress onto
individual sheets of Mohawk paper, then hand-adhered to a digipack-style paper sleeve.
While the hand illustrations create the feeling of a personal letter, the letterpress printing
creates a professional appearance so that the CD is still able to be sold if desired.

SF Independent Film Festival poster

Design: 17 Feet **Art Director:** Brandon Herring
Designer: Brandon Herring **Client:** San Francisco
Independent Film Festival **Materials:** paper bag, pencil,
ballpoint pen **Dimensions:** 24" x 36" (61cm x 91cm)

Comment: SF Indie has always been a do-it-yourself organization, so for their 2005 Independent Film Festival, we decided to highlight that sensibility. Instead of a red, glossy, ten-gallon bucket of popcorn, we used a simple brown bag with all the information for the festival handwritten. Nothing was computer generated. The type was sketched out in pencil, then traced with a ballpoint pen on a ten-cent bag. Using a large format camera to get dynamic perspective, the poster has an iconic presence, contrasting the humble nature of the actual creation and the final product, an inherent characteristic of the San Francisco Independent Film Festival. In the end, 2005 was the most successful turnout in their history.

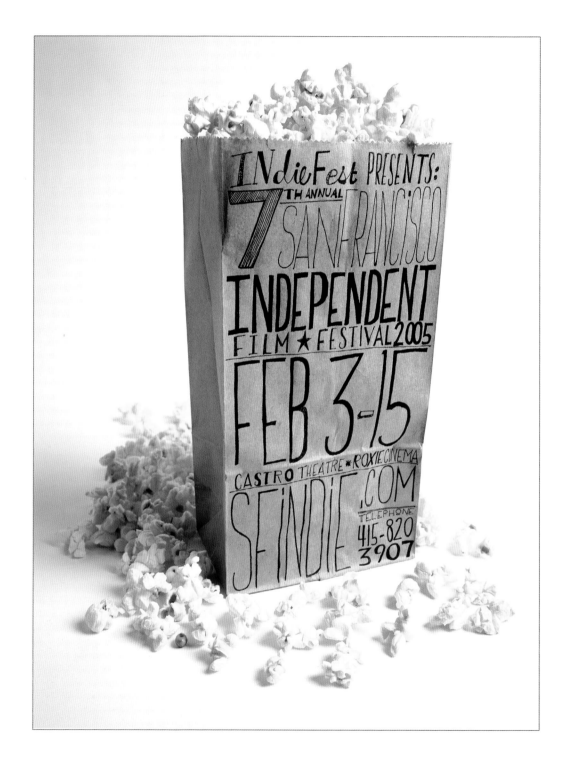

Pancho Sanchez record album

Design: The Creative Circus **Designer:** Ashley Hofman **Photographer:** Molly Vass **Materials:** silkscreen, tempera paint, cigar box

Comment: This album is the second in a series chronicling Sanchez' career in music. Titled "Vida" or "Life," the album cover was created using scans of the back of a cigar box and letters cut out of a tempera paint-soaked sponge.

0 2 2 FINGERPRINT

Transfer web site

Design: D5ive **Art Director:** Paul B. Drohan
Designer: Paul B. Drohan **Client:** Transfer
Band **Materials:** pencil, paper, copier, scanner,
computer

Comment: The web site for the band Transfer is a variety of things:
it's a resource for interested viewers to find up-to-date information,
band profiles, show dates and media resources. But most of all, it's an
extension of their brand. It carries the same feeling that the CDs, posters
and other materials have created. The use of abstract photography, hand
drawings, hand-lettering and scanned textures continues this aesthetic
throughout the site.

Phish summer tour tickets

Design: The Chopping Block **Art Director:** Matthew Richmond
Designer: Matthew Richmond **Client:** Phish

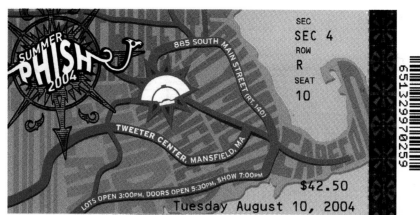

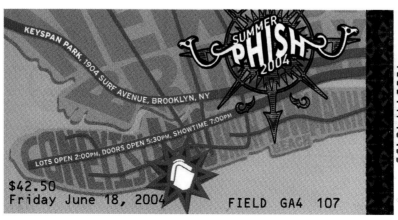

THREE HAIL ARNIES AND AN OUR HOGAN: A TRIP TO THE ETIQUETTE CONFESSIONAL

BY MICHAEL GRIFFITH

The silver cup resides in the understairs closet, amid other bric-a-brac: stained and time-warped racquets; a grocery sack filled with rope and twine; a host of half-sprung umbrellas we just might, in a pinch, bring out of retirement someday. There, on the high shelf to the right, next to a broken turntable trussed in its cord. The engraving is tarnished but still readable: *The William Allan Craig Sportsmanship Award, 1979.*

If you removed its bouquet of once-used paint stirrers and polished the silver, the cup might gleam impressively. But trophies lie.

———

Twenty-five years ago I was a fourteen-year-old golfer with mediocre skills and an aversion to practice. I was lucky enough to have unlimited access to a course, so I played often enough to have nudged my handicap down to ten. But I had no grand ambitions in golf. I was all too well aware of my limitations, physical and temperamental, and they weren't the kind that might one day suddenly vanish.

Illustration by Jeffrey Decoster

The Journal of the Shivas Irons Society

Design: Turner & Associates **Art Directors:** Stephen Turner, Tom Ingalls **Designers:** Kelly Conley, Ed O'Brien **Client:** The Shivas Iron Society **Materials:** pencil, pen, paint, scratchboard, computer **Printer:** Cenveo

Comment: *The Journal* is a literary and arts periodical, inspired by all things golf. Issue Two is an anthology of short stories, fiction, poetry, original art and historical artifacts that includes tobacco cards from the early twentieth century. The vision was to create a testament to the beauty and mystery of a game that too often is depicted through golf ball and real estate advertisements.

Yosemite National Park →
← Hoover Wilderness

END

Kyle Pierce self-promo

Design: Kyle Pierce Illustration
Designer: Kyle Pierce **Client:** Kyle
Pierce Illustration **Materials:** ink, oil
pastel, 120 mm film, Photoshop

Comment: There is no high-minded reason for the integration of handmade elements in my work, other than that I like to draw and take pictures and I found a way to harness both interests to one end. Occasionally, written text accompanies these "albums" as a means of layering stories and questioning the relatedness of seemingly disparate content. I begin by photographing an event, or series of events, then scan and edit the film or prints, keeping the chronology intact. The illustrated text and/or images are then layered onto the photos to create a second story.

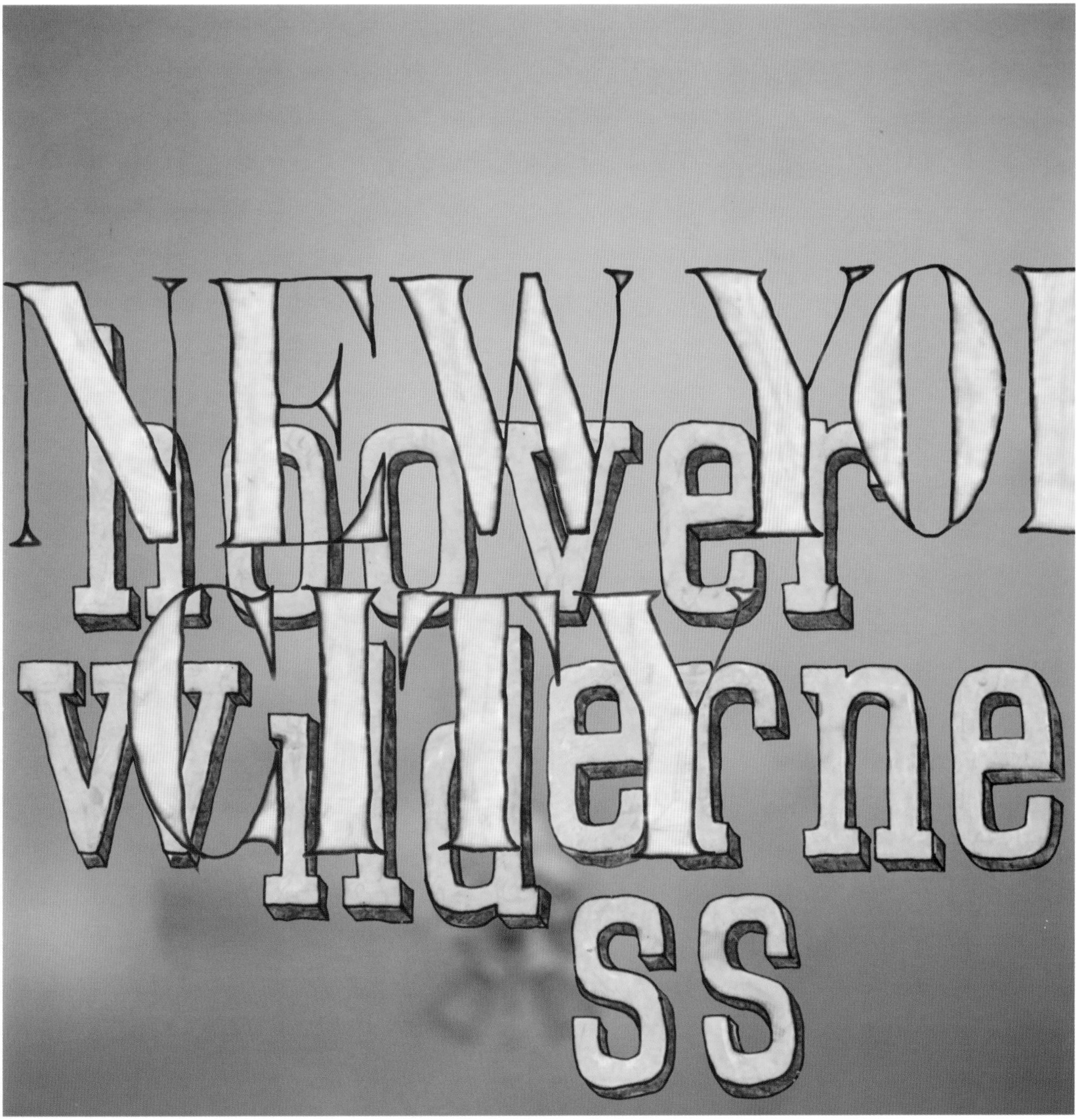
NEW YO
hover
wilderne
ss

The Letter H

From the time I was VERY LITTLE I loved to make Things. I made my own coloring books, I made my own paper dolls, I made dioramas, and I even made my own perfume by CRUSHING Rose petals into baby oil. I made barrette boxes out of POPSICLE STICKS, key chains out of lanyards, ashtrays out clay and Halloween costumes out of construction paper and old sheets. I grew up in a household with a strong "do it yourself" mentality and a MOM that made a living as a painter and a seamstress. SO I received a lot of acclaim from my family FOR MY ARTISTIC inclinations. I also found that making things by hand gave me a strong sense of accomplishment and PRIDE.

When I started Kindergarten an issue with my creative prowess EMERGED. Without any warning at all, AS I WAS FIRST LEARNING TO WRITE, it became CLEAR that I had trouble creating certain letterforms. I had specific Distress with the placement of the little TAIL on the CAPITAL Q. I also had difficulty discerning the lowercase b from the lowercase d (which was of particular concern, given my first name.) I ALSO had artistic AND intellectual RESISTANCE to the capital H. For some reason, I had trouble constructing two parallel lines crossed in the center by a horizontal one. I couldn't draw any of the lines STRAIGHT, I had trouble with the spatial relations between the vertical lines, and I was unable to get an even weight for the three markings. Looking back on it now I remember my mother getting so exasperated with me that she enlisted my grandmother to take over the doomed endeavor.

But as I continued to struggle, and my anguish turned to wrath, I experienced something that I had never consciously felt before: I couldn't do it. I couldn't make it right.

by Debbie Millman

While one might surmise the inability of a child to construct the letter H couldn't possibly have long-term ramifications, I must confess that all those years ago I was not called Debbie. I was called Deborah. And it was not spelled in the conventional manner: D-E-B-R-A. It was spelled D-E-B-O-R-A-H. Therefore, my inability to draw an H was rather worrisome. As my mighty efforts grew futile and my temper tantrum intensified over my many mangled H's, my inventive grandmother made a realization: since I had recently mastered my d's and b's, I would be able to spell Debbie! The name Deborah would no longer be an obstacle to my self-expression. And thus, a new moniker was established, and has lasted ever since.

It was in that instant I first fell in love with the agile, malleable and thoroughly magical acrobatics of typography, language and communication.

This tawdry affair has continued throughout my life. And I still have a preference for doing almost everything by hand. In a day and age when nano-technology and computer science have ushered in a brave new era, I believe there is a profound beauty in all things handmade. While computers might set type in flawlessly accurate columns, things that are made by hand are beautiful by virtue of their irregularity.

I see these imperfections as marks of dignity and integrity, and believe that they bear witness to the artist—and the human—in all of us.

Now all grown up, I have a fascination with any handmade object containing the written word. I find myself transformed by the collision of art and design inherent in the typographic missives of Ed Fella, Lawrence Weiner or Paula Scher and the heartbreaking handwritten narration in the work of Cy Twombly and Philip Guston. Even silly things such as tie-dyed T-shirts with dreamy messages like "Peace Now!" or a sadly optimistic "John Kerry in 2004" have this potency.

What resonates in these objects is an inherent authenticity and honesty.

What is contained in these objects is an enduring, uniquely human imprint. As we deconstruct our lives searching for meaning, it is these handcrafted messages that have the magnitude—and the permanence—to measure, reflect and express who we are.

I recently came upon one the most ambitious projects I undertook as a young adult: a completely handwritten, hand drawn magazine that I did in collaboration with my best friend, also named Debbie. In honor of our efforts and our teenage aspirations we named it Debutante. **We made sure the title didn't contain an** *H.*

02

ILLUSTRATION

The visual communication of an idea
or an object is executed, at least in part,
by someone with exemplary powers of observation—
and the ability to translate those observations
into meaningful hand-articulated forms.

Muse poster

Design: Ames Bros **Designer:** Barry Ament
Client: House of Blues/Smokestack **Materials:**
pencil, paper, computer **Printer:** Seribellum
Dimensions: 11½" x 23" (29cm x 58cm)

Comment: We worked on a series of posters for the House of Blues back in 2004. Often, there wasn't a design budget at all, so I would try to knock a poster out in a day—tip to tail, separations for film, the whole nine yards. The beauty of approaching a project like this is that it's raw and unpolished and usually better than something that takes weeks. The band has dark lyrics—most every song referring to the end of the world—so I wanted to capture that dark side with the subject matter but play to the melodic side of the music with color and technique. The final poster was silk-screened using two colors.

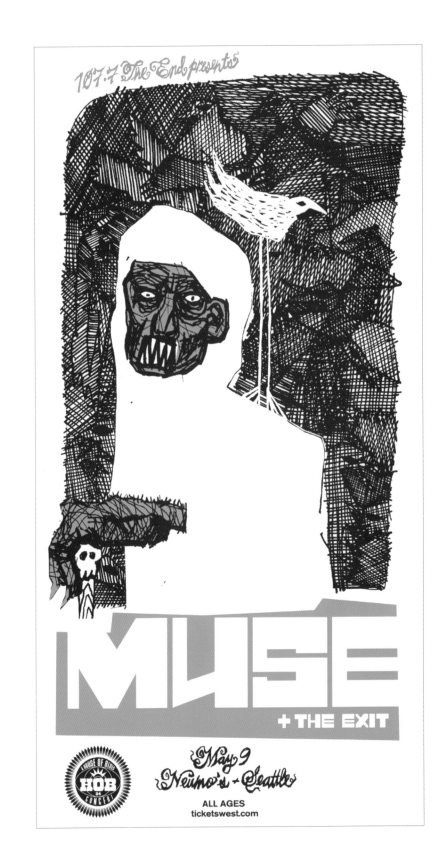

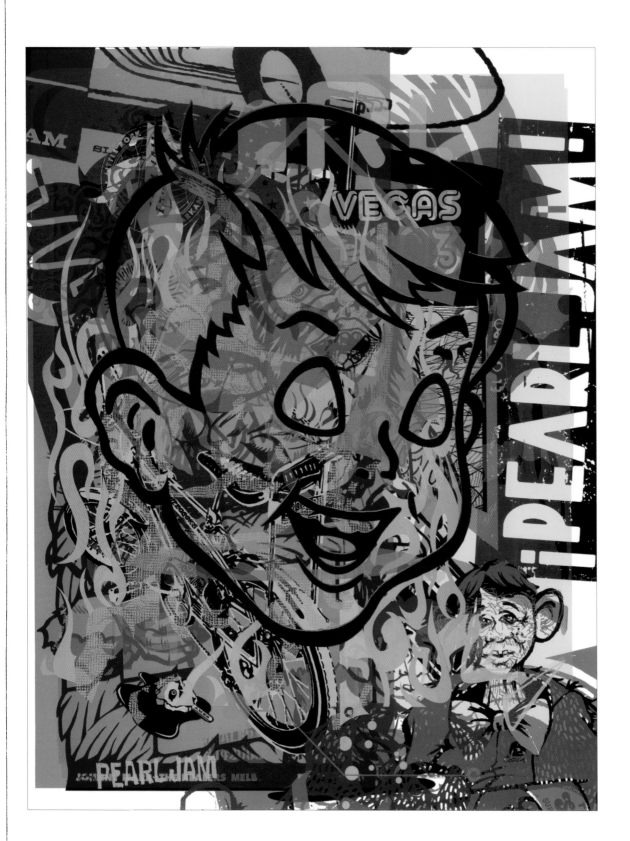

Ames Bros test print

Design: Ames Bros **Designers:** Barry
Ament, Coby Schultz **Client:** Ames Bros
Materials: pen, ink **Printer:** Seribellum
Dimensions: 20" x 26" (51cm x 66cm)

COMMENT: We have the best darn screen printer this world has ever known . . . one Mr. Joe Barela. Joe is an artist himself and a great thing that he does is take our artwork and reinterpret it by layering artwork from different posters as he's printing. Often times these are three or four year odysseys with a dozen posters and dozens of colors. Thick and juicy. Some call these test prints—we like to think of them as pieces of art. In fact, this is the only thing we've ever designed that I have hanging in my house and every time I walk by it I see something new. Tons of colors in this one.

AIGA Design Conference, Boston

Design: 344 Design, LLC Designer: Stefan G. Bucher
Client: STEP Inside Design

Comment: This is an illustrated reporting and commentary about the 2005 AIGA National Design Conference in Boston. This piece was influenced by the work of R. Crumb, Art Spiegelman, Chris Ware, Rube Goldberg, Norman Schureman and Matt Groening.

Comment: Chill & Spill is a journal designed for teens that have experienced trauma and need a place to voice their feelings. Because we wanted to encourage the kids to explore their own artistic hand, the illustrations had to have a rougher, handmade quality that would inspire, rather than discourage them. We chose twenty-one illustrators based on their track record of success with MTV, *Rolling Stone*, Levi Jeans, Sony Records. Andrew Wicklund's hand-drawn headlines and Mark Todd's imperfectly doodled title created a perfect invitation for teens to express themselves.

Chill & Spill journal

Design: Art With Heart Art Director: Steffanie Lorig Designer: Andrew Wicklund Client: Art With Heart Materials: mixed media, collage, etc.
Printer: Hemlock

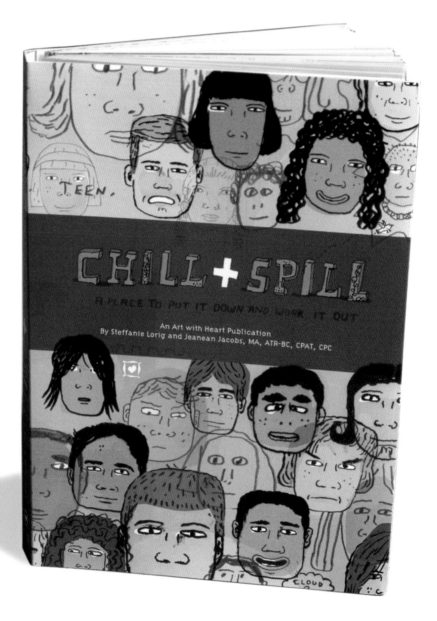

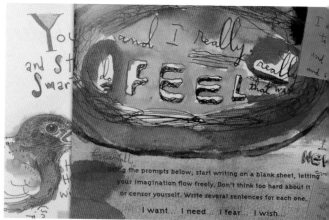

Using the prompts below, start writing on a blank sheet, letting your imagination flow freely. Don't think too hard about it or censor yourself. Write several sentences for each one.

I want... I need... I fear... I wish...

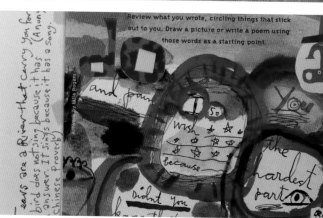

Review what you wrote, circling things that stick out to you. Draw a picture or write a poem using those words as a starting point.

Designer: Mario Suter **Materials:** pencil, ink and coal **Printer:** Ueaendruck, Wzern **Dimensions:** 11¾" x 16½" (30cm x 42cm)

Comment: I made this poster for one of a series of Postrock concerts in 2005. Postrock is an experimental form of rock music and the band itself was the inspiration for the poster. To create the artwork I just listened to the band's music and drew using coal, pencil and ink. The goal was for the final offset print to retain as much of the original illustration's handmade quality as possible.

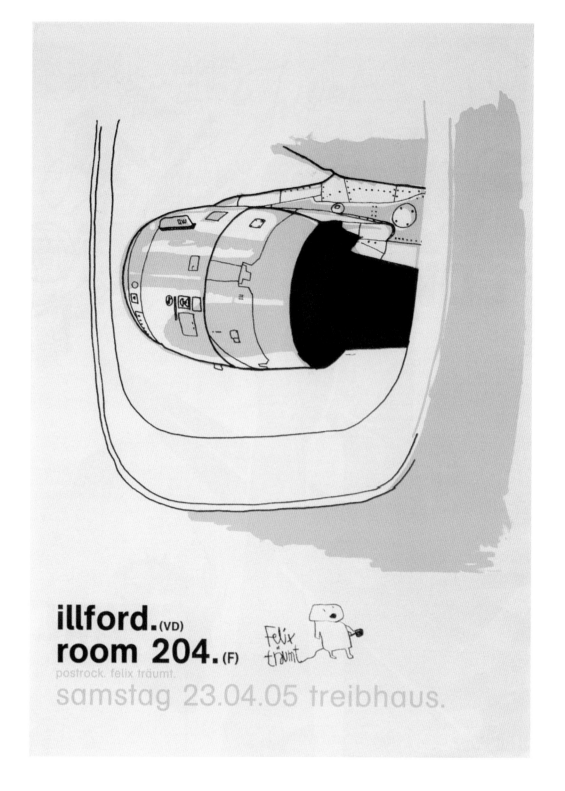

Comment: The band All The Pretty Horses has a sense of humor that blurs the lines of music, sexuality and performance art. Building on this, we came up with the image of a dual-headed male horse wearing mascara. This hand-inked illustration is layered over a bleeding bright red heart sliding down the page. The illustration was transferred directly to the screens and hand-printed in limited quantity for the show. No computers were involved.

All The Pretty Horses poster

Design: Planet Propaganda **Art Director:** Kevin Wade
Designer: Kevin Wade **Client:** High Noon Saloon
Materials: screen printing **Printer:** Planet Propaganda
Dimensions: 19" x 25" (48cm x 64cm)

Chrome Dome

Or, how I learned to stop worrying and love the shine!

INSPIRATION

PRODUCTS

HOW TO SHAVE

HORROR STORIES

←BEFORE

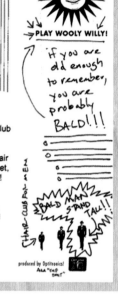

PLAY WOOLY WILLY!

If you are old enough to remember, you are probably BALD!!!

HAIR CLUB FOR MEN

BALD MAN STAND TALL!!

produced by Optitronics! A.k.a "THE SHIT"

HORROR STORIES

Bald Men Look!

Sticky goo!

TRAPPED!

Above is my first "Glued on Rug". How disgusting! I joined the Hair Club For Men where, for about $250 a month, plus services, tipping and products, it reached around $320 a month!! I joined this program thinking wow, those guys on TV have a really great looking head of hair and it looks so real, girls run their hands through it, water ski, get it wet, ect.ect. I want everyone out there to know all that stuff is pure BULL!! I've tried dating a few girls and yes eventually they will find out, and they will be so pissed that you never told them about it! That is the bottom line fellas!!!! They will eventually find out! And they will dump your ass!! Anyway, listen to Chrome Dome and don't get a rug!! I feel trapped to this glued on mess! Help!

-Guy Miloan, Virginia Beach, VA

Chrome Dome

Or, how I learned to stop worrying and love the shine!

INSPIRATION

PRODUCTS

HOW TO SHAVE

HORROR STORIES

←BEFORE

PLAY WOOLY WILLY!

If you are old enough to remember, you are probably BALD!!!

HAIR CLUB FOR MEN

BALD MAN STAND TALL!!

produced by Optitronics! A.k.a "THE SHIT"

HOW TO SHAVE

Bald Men Grow Hair Quick!

bullshit!

SHAVING TIPS!

• Take a hot shower before you shave. It relaxes the pores and makes it easier to shave.

• Use a clean, new razor, and shaving cream. See "products" page for suggested razors and shaving cream.

• Avoid shaving against the grain and shave in the direction that your hair grows (or used to grow).

• Aftershave should be used to avoid rashes.

• The absolute best way to shave your head is to ask your wife or girlfriend to do it. They love to do it and it feels good.

• Use Aloe Vera lotion to keep that young healthy look and don't forget your sun block if your going to be in sun.

• If you want to try Nair or Magic, you must be stupid. Don't leave it on any longer than recommended, otherwise it burns.

INSPIRATION

PRODUCTS

HOW TO SHAVE

HORROR STORIES

Chrome Dome web site

Design: SVA MFA Design School **Art Director:** Chris Capuozzo **Designer:** Brian E Smith **Materials:** pen, paper, scanner

Comment: Chrome Dome is a project, done in good humor, to offer resources to encourage men who are balding not to succumb to the lure of toupees, hair plugs and the like. I researched many images online of men wearing toupees in search for Chrome Dome's mascot. Once I found him, I was reminded of the days when I would receive fashion catalogs addressed to the former resident of my apartment. My friends and I would draw all over their faces to alter the image they portrayed of being slick, well-dressed and respected fashion models.

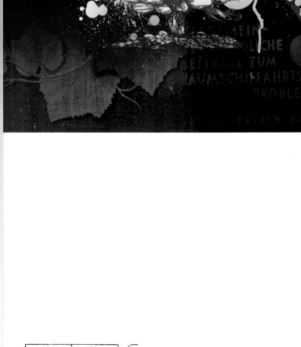

Exopolis book prints

Design: Exopolis **Art Director:** Jorge Calleja **Designer:** Jorge Calleja

Comment: As time goes by, I feel the need to bring handmade elements into my comps. I guess it's just nostalgia speaking through my tablet. I feel the need to detach myself from the virtual world and incorporate some spark of reality into my designs. In these comps I see a lot of Mexican and European influences on my life; the woman flying over Paris and the MexiCola. It's a merging of the Hispanic-American world I have been living in lately: dirty, crowded, rustic, and merchandised. I think it says to not be too serious, to just enjoy the ride.

ILLUSTRATION

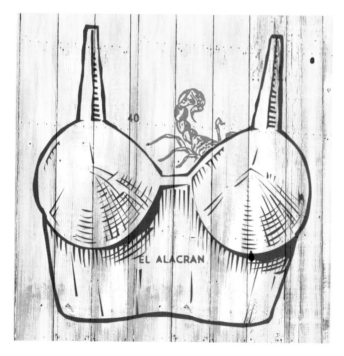

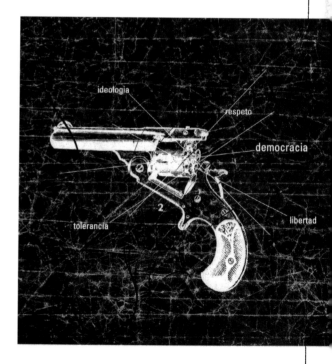

Luna poster

Design: Ames Bros **Designer:** Coby Schultz
Client: Neumos/Smokestack **Materials:**
fabric, X-acto knife **Printer:** Patent Pending

Comment: Luna has a decent underground following. My initial reaction to the music was that it had kind of a slow-moving peacefulness. I found a cool midcentury tapestry image and started thinking of different things I could illustrate in that style that would encompass the band. A bird seemed like a logical step, so I used some burlap, linen and different fabric textures, and wielded my X-acto blade and glue stick with a fashion and efficiency that would've made my junior high crafts teacher proud. The outcome was something full of dimension that every generation can enjoy.

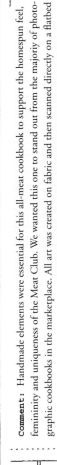

Comment: Handmade elements were essential for this all-meat cookbook to support the homespun feel, femininity and uniqueness of the Meat Club. We wanted this one to stand out from the majority of photographic cookbooks in the marketplace. All art was created on fabric and then scanned directly on a flatbed scanner. The design and illustrations combine vintage fabrics, stitching, iron-on transfers and painting. Vintage meat illustrations and various fabric trimmings add to the book's character. Each gatefold contains an embroidered cow, sheep and pig divided into parts to give an easy and fun way to learn.

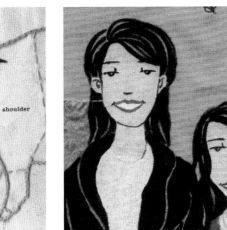

Meat Club cookbook

Design: Chronicle Books   Designer: Vanessa Dina
client: Chronicle Books   Materials: iron-on transfer, fabric, paint, trimmings, threads

ILLUSTRATION

Okaydave portfolio

Design: Okay Samurai Multimedia **Art Director:** Dave Werner **Designer:** Dave Werner **Client:** Okay Samurai Multimedia **Materials:** cardboard, coffee-stained paper, wacom tablet, computer

Comment: This portfolio was meant to show not only a diverse collection of work, but my thinking process and personality as well. Hand-drawn notes float in and out of place while short movies accompany each piece to reveal the stories behind the finished products. Every project—from an online interactive novel called *Cadence of Seasons* to a futuristic portable coffee machine—started with pencil and paper. Rather than hiding those origins, this concept-driven portfolio celebrates them.

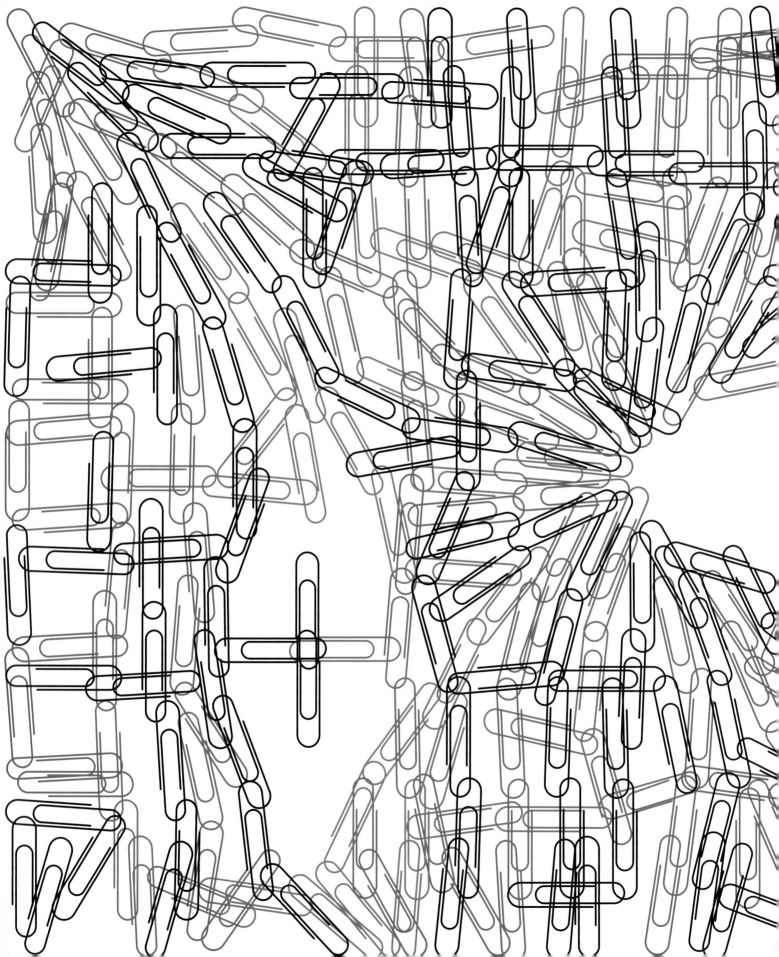

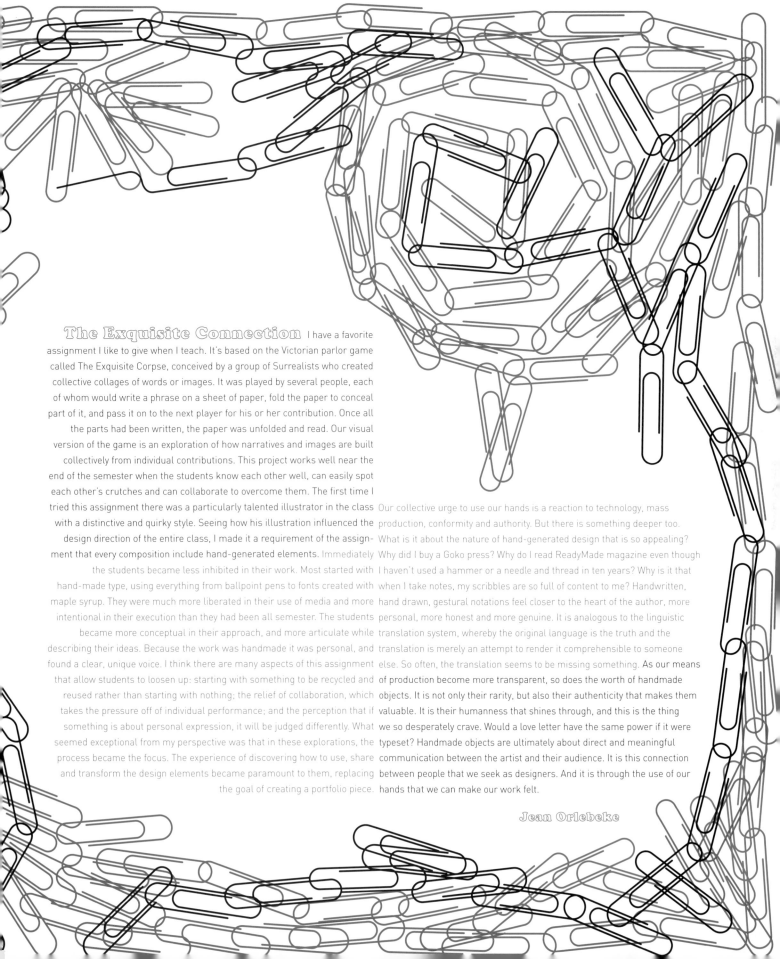

The Exquisite Connection I have a favorite assignment I like to give when I teach. It's based on the Victorian parlor game called The Exquisite Corpse, conceived by a group of Surrealists who created collective collages of words or images. It was played by several people, each of whom would write a phrase on a sheet of paper, fold the paper to conceal part of it, and pass it on to the next player for his or her contribution. Once all the parts had been written, the paper was unfolded and read. Our visual version of the game is an exploration of how narratives and images are built collectively from individual contributions. This project works well near the end of the semester when the students know each other well, can easily spot each other's crutches and can collaborate to overcome them. The first time I tried this assignment there was a particularly talented illustrator in the class with a distinctive and quirky style. Seeing how his illustration influenced the design direction of the entire class, I made it a requirement of the assignment that every composition include hand-generated elements. Immediately the students became less inhibited in their work. Most started with hand-made type, using everything from ballpoint pens to fonts created with maple syrup. They were much more liberated in their use of media and more intentional in their execution than they had been all semester. The students became more conceptual in their approach, and more articulate while describing their ideas. Because the work was handmade it was personal, and found a clear, unique voice. I think there are many aspects of this assignment that allow students to loosen up: starting with something to be recycled and reused rather than starting with nothing; the relief of collaboration, which takes the pressure off of individual performance; and the perception that if something is about personal expression, it will be judged differently. What seemed exceptional from my perspective was that in these explorations, the process became the focus. The experience of discovering how to use, share and transform the design elements became paramount to them, replacing the goal of creating a portfolio piece.

Our collective urge to use our hands is a reaction to technology, mass production, conformity and authority. But there is something deeper too. What is it about the nature of hand-generated design that is so appealing? Why did I buy a Goko press? Why do I read ReadyMade magazine even though I haven't used a hammer or a needle and thread in ten years? Why is it that when I take notes, my scribbles are so full of content to me? Handwritten, hand drawn, gestural notations feel closer to the heart of the author, more personal, more honest and more genuine. It is analogous to the linguistic translation system, whereby the original language is the truth and the translation is merely an attempt to render it comprehensible to someone else. So often, the translation seems to be missing something. As our means of production become more transparent, so does the worth of handmade objects. It is not only their rarity, but also their authenticity that makes them valuable. It is their humanness that shines through, and this is the thing we so desperately crave. Would a love letter have the same power if it were typeset? Handmade objects are ultimately about direct and meaningful communication between the artist and their audience. It is this connection between people that we seek as designers. And it is through the use of our hands that we can make our work felt.

Jean Orlebeke

03

MIXED MESSAGES

The sum of the parts is greater than the whole.
Visual layering echoes the never-simple nature of life
with its multiple levels, rich textures and often ragged edges.
Without the participation of the pieces,
no puzzle would ever be solved.

Beneath the Surface skate deck

Design: Simeon Man Kreative **Art Director:**
Allan S. Manzano **Designer:** Allan S. Manzano
Client: Simeon Man Kreative **Materials:** skate-
board (wood), recycled magazines, resin

Comment: The skate deck project was designed to show the creative
process I undergo before I tackle any design job. Whether it is using
trash or recycled goods, I always try to reinvent so that nothing goes to
waste. For me, it was all about the process of getting my hands dirty and
seeing how a piece of aluminum is reinterpreted into a new form with new
patterns of type and composition. When I'm stuck or clueless about
solving a design problem, I turn to the basics of handmade projects.

Scapes magazine illustration

Design: The Design Bureau of Amerika **Art Director:** Keith Bowman **Designer:** Keith Bowman **Client:** Scapes **Materials:** mixed media

Comment: This piece was used as an illustration for an article about growing up in the 1970s for the 'zine *Scapes*. It was important that the finished piece felt like it could have been created in the 1970s and didn't have any digital feel to it. Most of the graphics were hand-drawn in black ink onto paper that we purposely distressed and stained. The color was added in ink and gouache onto separate sheets of paper. Some type was hand-lettered while the rest used a font that was created from my handwriting.

PIXIES SELL OUT

PRODUCED BY MICHEAL & BOROFSKY

LIVE AT EUROKEENES FESTIVAL: BELFORT, FRANCE

1. BONE MACHINE
2. WAVE OF MUTILATION (SURF)
3. SOMETHING AGAINST YOU
4. RIVER EUPHRATES
5. U-MASS
6. BONE MACHINE
7. CACTUS
8. ED IS DEAD
9. I BLEED
10. MONKEY GONE TO HEAVEN
11. HEY
12. LEVITATE ME
13. SUBBACULTCHA
14. DEAD
15. GOUGE AWAY
16. VELOURIA
17. MR. GRIEVES
18. CRACKITY JONES
19. BROKEN FACE
20. ISLA DE ENCANTA
21. TAME
22. HERE COMES YOUR MAN
23. VELOURIA
24. WHERE IS MY MIND?
25. VAMOS
26. WAVE OF MUTILATION
27. GIGANTIC
28. VELOURIA

BONUS TRACKS

1. MONKEY GONE TO HEAVEN*
2. PLANET OF SOUND*
3. HERE COMES YOUR MAN*
4. WHERE IS MY MIND?*
5. NIMROD'S SON*
6. THE HOLIDAY SONG*
7. No. 13 BABY**
8. CARIBOU**
9. DEBASER***
10. SUBBACULTCHA***
11. VAMOS***
12. IS SHE WEIRD*†
13. U-MASS*†
14. CRACKITY JONES*
15. INTO THE WHITE**
16. GIGANTIC**

* From The Move Festival: Manchester, England
† From Voodoo Festival: New Orleans, LA
‡ From Fuji Rock Festival: Naeba, Japan
** From Tsongas Arena: Lowell, MA
*† From Coachella: Indio, CA
*** From T In The Park: Edinburgh, Scotland
*** From Austin City Limits Festival: Austin, TX

CBLOR/ XX MINUTES

BONUS FEATURES:

PCM

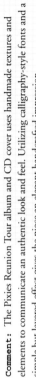

Comment: The Pixies Reunion Tour album and CD cover uses handmade textures and elements to communicate an authentic look and feel. Utilizing calligraphy-style fonts and a simple but layered effect gives the piece an elegant handcrafted impression.

Pixies Reunion Tour CD packaging

Design: The Chopping Block **Art Director:** Thomas Romer **Designer:** Thiago Demello Bueno **Client:** The Pixies / Rhino Records

Shutter poster

Design: University of Nebraska-Kearney **Art Director:** Joel Kreutzer **Designer:** Joel Kreutzer **Client:** University of Nebraska-Kearney **Materials:** Illustrator, Photoshop, photocopier, hand-distressed

Comment: The demise of the avant-garde filmmaker: the message in this poster is probably the most simplified and direct of our poster series. The bold image of a person's face is used to communicate the idea that this film is focused more on the individuals of the film industry than film itself. The Xs over the eyes, representing death, is not an original idea, but it's still a device that works well symbolically. Using film strips to create the Xs adds a new twist. The look and colors of the poster came from the notion of these experimental filmmakers using handmade elements and film chemicals to manipulate and create a new art form.

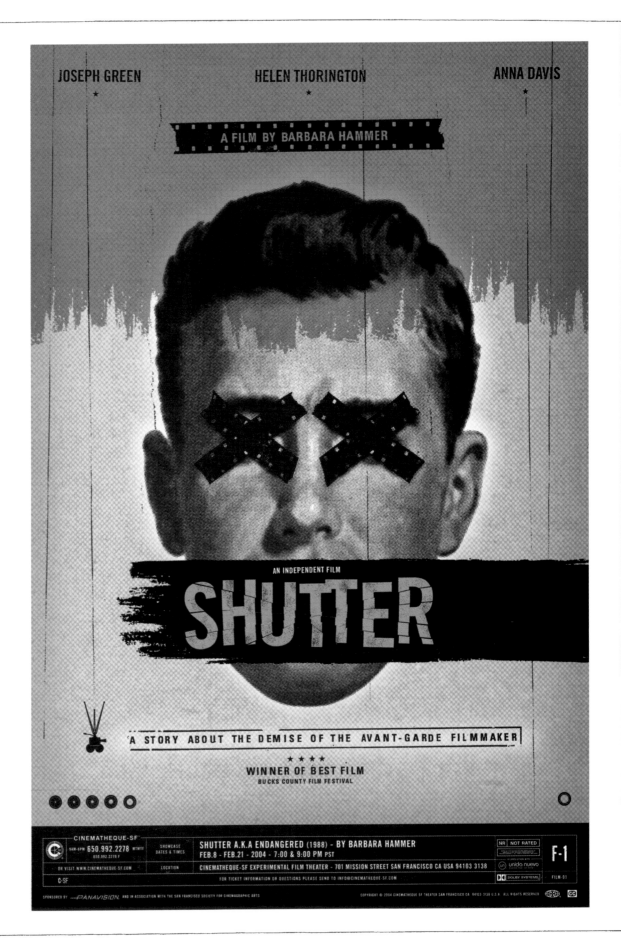

Mental Radio poster

Design: University of Nebraska-Kearney **Art Director:** Joel Kreutzer **Designer:** Joel Kreutzer **Client:** University of Nebraska-Kearney **Materials:** Illustrator, Photoshop, photocopier, hand-distressed

Comment: This poster is essentially designed in two parts, split down the middle, and produces the same awkward reaction that comes from viewing the film itself. The story documents two telepathic individuals. One person sits in a private room and sketches an image from her head. The other person translates that image onto paper from another room using telepathy; the results are surprisingly similar. The illustrations of the two chairs are actual images from these studies. The background pattern, which looks like old wallpaper, connotes that these studies were done in an ordinary home, not a laboratory.

The True and the Questions journal

Design: Chronicle Books **Art Director:** Kristen Hewitt
Designer: Sabrina Ward Harrison, Kristen Hewitt **Client:**
Chronicle Books **Materials:** mixed media

Comment: This journal encourages users to write, draw, paint, collage and make messes creatively to get to the heart of their lives and souls. Sabrina created over fifty pieces of collaged artwork, many of which became the backgrounds for the journal pages. The art was then photographed digitally so the dimension and texture of the collages would shine through. Handwritten text gives the feeling that Sabrina is guiding the user through the journal experience.

A Handmade Life

Love it all.
THE FEAR
THE EXCITEMENT
THE POWER
THE UNWORTHINESS
FEELINGS
THE ANGER

read
Mary
Oliver
poems

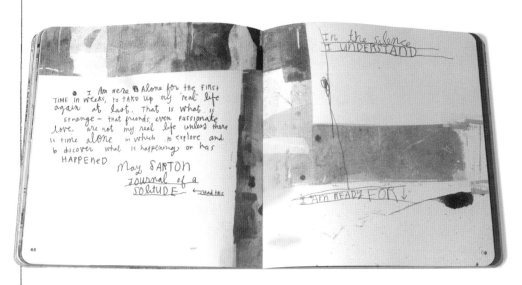

• I AM HERE Alone for the FIRST TIME in weeks, to TAKE up my 'real' life again at last. That is what is strange — that friends, even passionate love, are not my real life unless there is time alone in which to explore and to discover what is happening or has HAPPENED May SARTON
JOURNAL of a
SOLITUDE read this

In the silence
I UNDERSTAND

I AM READY FOR

El Champions of Justice poster / cards

Design: The Design Bureau of Amerika **Art Director:** Keith Bowman **Designer:** Keith Bowman **Client:** Konsumer Goods **Materials:** mixed media

Comment: El Champions of Justice is a limited run of trading cards that is a parody/tribute to the Mexican masked wrestlers of the 1960s and 1970s. The featured wrestlers are fictional, but the client wanted to mimic the hand-drawn simplicity of the event posters found on the streets of Mexico. Each wrestler was hand-drawn and inked, then carved into linoleum blocks for printing onto newsprint. Colors were created by mixing acrylics with linseed oil and were then brushed onto various types of paper. Silkscreened illustrations and collage were also incorporated. When the cards are put together in order, the backsides form the image of the poster.

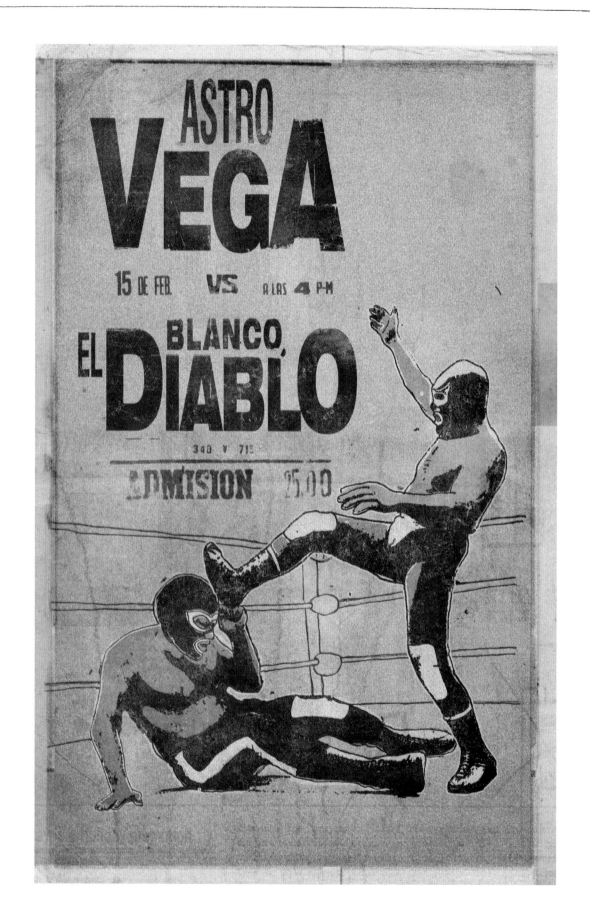

EL MASKED MONK

BLUE ZOMBIE JR.

Piper Warlick identity system

Designer: Ashley Hofman **Client:** Piper Warlick
Materials: old postage marks, vintage women's hat catalogs, fishnet stockings

Comment: This identity system was for a photographer who specializes in shooting women in 1940s vintage costumes in an old Hollywood studio style format. The mark was developed by combining the elements of old postmarks and messing with images found in old women's hat catalogs from the 1930s and 1940s. A pair of fishnet stockings was scanned to finish the piece.

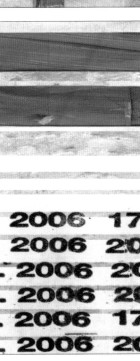

Comment: My work is based on rubbish (pieces of paper, old color, etc.) lying around in my studio or that is collected in boxes. This poster was composed using acrylic color on paper with cut out pieces of my old work. All the red and green typography is cut out of a white background, so you can see the red texture. The black typography is nitro-technik. After making the original, I scanned it and copied some parts of the background.

Molière: Der Geizige poster

Design: Luca Schenardi Art Director: Luca Schenardi
Designer: Luca Schenardi Client: Theater Momänt & Co.
Materials: acrylic, collage Printer: Gasser-Druck, Erstfeld

Slacker DVD packaging

Design: Marc English Design **Art Director:** Marc English
Designers: Michael Nowlin, Bart Kubbe, Mindy McCracken, Marc English, Rebecka English **Client:** The Criterion Collection
Materials: foam core, duct tape, spray paint, socket wrench, etc.

Comment: Richard Linklater's cult film, *Slacker,* is of the streets. Over the course of twenty-four hours, it weaves in and out of a variety of scenarios in the most tangential of manners. The environments become as essential to the film as the characters. There is enough do-it-yourself attitude throughout the film to warrant a treatment that encompasses evidence of this attitude—from the house numbers on curbs, to handwritten notepads left on dirty dishes, to flyers on telephone poles.

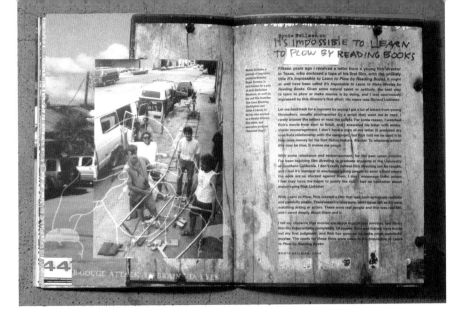

Monte Hellman on
IT'S IMPOSSIBLE TO LEARN TO PLOW BY READING BOOKS

Monte Hellman, a protégé of legendary auteur/director Roger Corman, is best known for a pair of Jack Nicholson Westerns, as well as the cult film favorites Two-Lane Blacktop, Cockfighter, and China 9 Liberty 37. He has also worked as theater director, film editor, and executive producer (Reservoir Dogs).

Fifteen years ago I received a letter from a young film director in Texas, who enclosed a tape of his first film, with the unlikely title *It's Impossible to Learn to Plow by Reading Books*. It might as well have been called *It's Impossible to Learn to Make Movies by Reading Books*. Given some natural talent or aptitude, the best way to learn to plow or make movies is by doing, and I was enormously impressed by this director's first effort. His name was Richard Linklater.

Let me backtrack for a moment by saying I get a lot of letters from young filmmakers, usually accompanied by a script they want me to read. I rarely answer the letters or read the scripts. For some reason, I watched Rick's movie from start to finish, and I answered his letter with enthusiastic encouragement. I don't have a copy of my letter (it predated my love/hate relationship with the computer), but Rick told me he used it to help raise money for his first 35mm feature, *Slacker*. To whatever extent this may be true, it makes me proud.

With some reluctance and embarrassment, for the past seven months I've been teaching film directing to graduate students at the University of Southern California. I don't exactly believe film directing can be taught, and I feel it's immoral to encourage young people to enter a field where the odds are so stacked against them. I don't encourage them unless I feel they have the talent to justify the risk. I had no hesitation about encouraging Rick Linklater.

With *Learn to Plow*, Rick created a film that was both extremely realistic and painfully poetic. There wasn't a false note, and I never felt as if I were watching acting or actors. These were real people and this was real life, and I cared deeply about them and it.

I tell my students that movies are about anguish and emotion, and Rick's film fits these artists completely. Of course, time and history have borne out my first judgment, and Rick has gone on to make some wonderful movies. The seeds for these films were sown in *It's Impossible to Learn to Plow by Reading Books*.

MONTE HELLMAN, 2004

> ...this
> town has
> always
> had it's
> share of
> crazies,
> wouldn't
> want to
> live...

...and remember, the passion for destruction is...

...Texas is full of those so-called modern-day Libertarians, with all their goddamn selfish individualism. Just the opposite of real anarchism. They don't give a damn about improving the world...

- STEAL T...
- STEAL T...
- DEMAN...
- TRICK O...
- IT WILL BE GOOD
- TACO AND A HALF AFTER TEN
- PUT IT ON THE SHELL CARD
- IT'S A MAYONAISE COMMERCIAL
- WE ARE SPIRALING IN
- BACK TO ONE
- THE PERFECT RUN THROUGH
- WORK IN PROGRESS
- GIANT CAPPACINNO

...end of interview...

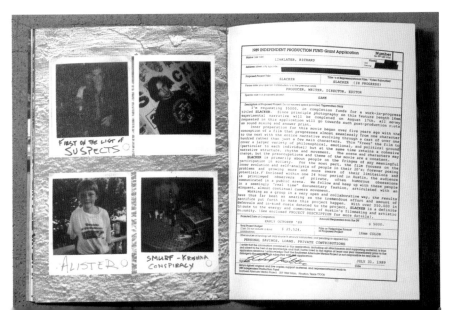

FIRST ON THE LIST OF SUSPECTS

ALISTER

SMURF - KRISHNA CONSPIRACY

1989 INDEPENDENT PRODUCTION FUND Grant Application

Name: LINKLATER, RICHARD

Proposed Project Title: SLACKER — Title of Representational Film/Video Submitted: SLACKER (IN PROGRESS)

Please state your special contributions to the previous work: PRODUCER, WRITER, DIRECTOR, EDITOR

Specify roles in proposed project: SAME

Description of Proposed Project:

I'm requesting $5000. in completion funds for a work-in-progress titled SLACKER. Since principle photography on this feature length 16mm experimental narrative will be completed on August 17th, all money requested in this application will go towards such post-production costs as sound mixing and answer print.

Inner preparation for this movie began over five years ago with the conception of a film that progresses almost seamlessly from one character to the next with the entire narrative evolving through a cast of over one hundred rather than just a few main characters. This "frees" the film to cover a larger variety of philosophical, emotional, and political ground (particular to each individual) but at the same time retains a cohesive narrative structure, rhythm and movement.

SLACKER is primarily about people on the fringes of any meaningful participation in society. For the most part, the film focuses on the inner evolution and self-analysis of people in their 20's; forever posing problems and growing more and more aware of their limitations and potentials. Enclosed within one 24 hour period in Austin, the audience is privileged observers of private, often humorous obsessions communicated in a seemingly "real time" documentary fashion, articulated with an eloquent, almost continual camera movement.

Working as a group in a very open and collaborative way, the results have thus far been as amazing as the tremendous effort and amount of sacrifice put forth to make this project happen. With over $50,000 in deferrals and in-kind costs donated to the project, SLACKER is a definite tribute to the energy and commitment of Austin's filmmaking and artistic community. (See enclosed PROJECT DESCRIPTION for more details).

Projected Date of Completion: EARLY OCTOBER '89

Total Project Budget: $25,524. — Amount Requested from the IPF: $5000.

Film or Videotape Format of Proposed Project: 16mm COLOR

PERSONAL SAVINGS, LOANS, PRIVATE CONTRIBUTIONS

JULY 31, 1989

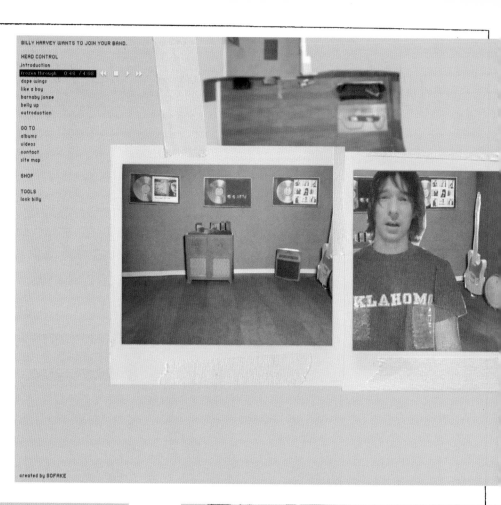

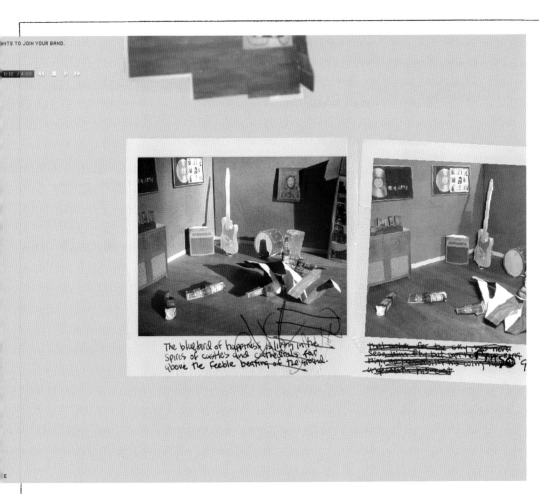

The bluebird of happiness is living in the spires of castles and cathedrals far above the feeble beating of the ground.

Billy Harvey web site

Design: sofake **Art Director:** Jordan Stone
Designer: Jordan Stone **Client:** Billy Harvey
Materials: paper, scissors, tape

Comment: Aging rock star Billy Harvey needed a web site and I needed the money. After a week of using powerful narcotics together, I vaguely remember printing Billy out and making a little diorama of his living room. I played out his life for him, printing new characters as needed. Right before I passed out I said, "Billy, every living thing on this earth will one day face death alone." I woke up three days later, took photographs of the pieces and made the site.

I'VE BEEN ASKED TO WRITE AN ESSAY FOR THIS BOOK
by Martin Venezky

I've been asked to write an essay for this book. Weeks
have passed and I have nothing to show. Why am I so
reluctant? I've lectured on the subject of handcraft
often enough, and defended its value to my students and
colleagues. The problem is neither the words nor my
persuasive skill. Most likely, it is the permanence of
the text. An author writes to construct an argument.
Deliberate, scholarly, assured, the thoughts form a
straight line. Publishing these words commits them to
scrutiny. And just assembling this first paragraph is
causing me to backtrack in panic.

If I had been asked to draw instead of write, I
would have filled pages without effort. There is a direct
fluid response from my brain to my hand to pen and paper.
But that well worn channel seems to circumvent language.
It's not that I can't write down words. Several pages in
my notebook have already been devoted to thoughts for this
essay. But those thoughts are then embellished with
drawing. The lines frame the words, dividing the pages
into geographic zones. Drawing sews these territories
together and embroiders over them, sometimes dominating
them beyond recognition.

This is not such a rare thing for those inclined
to visual work. But for me, the odd thing is that the
drawing is almost always abstract. Not doodles, but organic
structure. One line leads to the next. I'll see an
accumulation of marks and automatically swerve the mass
to one side. One division decrees that four more be
born, and so on. If these decisions are conscious,
which they probably are, I make them so quickly that I
can't record them in words. And that's a good thing.
Others may disagree, but for me these meandering drawings
aren't a symptom of inattention. They are simultaneous
to my listening, like a channel that produces no inter-
ference.

If my goal was to faithfully render something
observed, I would find myself evaluating every mark for
its fidelity and truth. That dialogue would fill up my
head, killing the flow, and shattering my concentration.
When my drawn lines insist on wrapping themselves around
an outside thought, type is their structure of choice.
I guess the alphabet's inherent abstraction is a natural
fit for my mark making. After all, a letterform is an
organizational system--an abstraction whose relationship
conform to a cultural understanding. (How tenuous
the understanding--or how specific the culture--is one of
the jolliest issues of design and communication.)

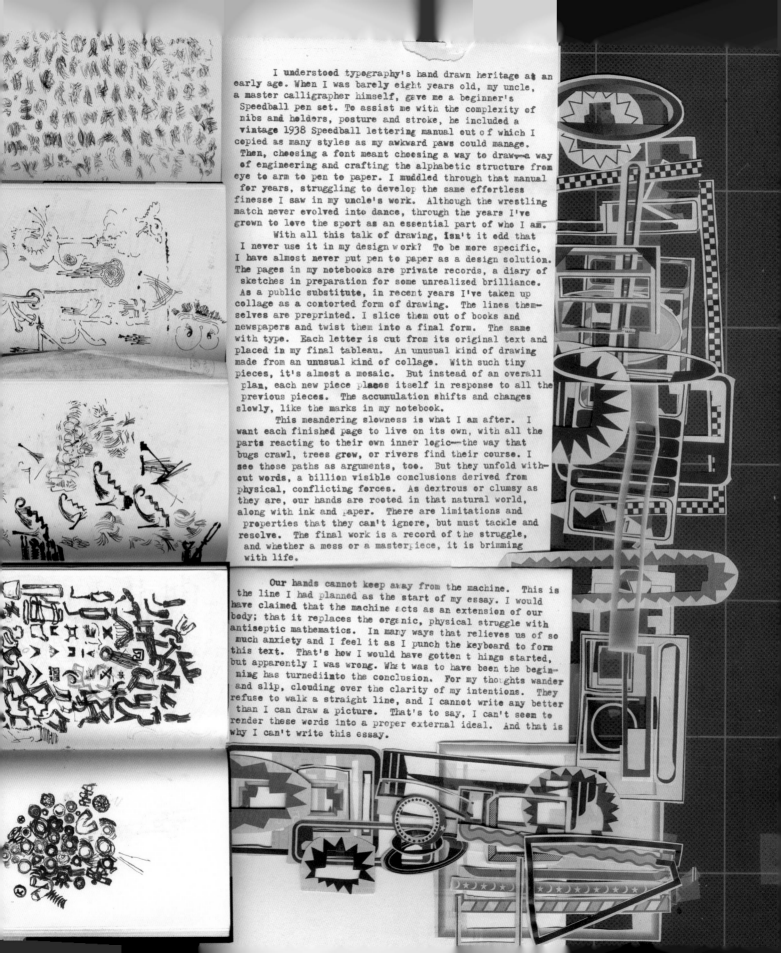

I understood typography's hand drawn heritage at an early age. When I was barely eight years old, my uncle, a master calligrapher himself, gave me a beginner's Speedball pen set. To assist me with the complexity of nibs and holders, posture and stroke, he included a vintage 1938 Speedball lettering manual out of which I copied as many styles as my awkward paws could manage. Then, choosing a font meant choosing a way to draw—a way of engineering and crafting the alphabetic structure from eye to arm to pen to paper. I muddled through that manual for years, struggling to develop the same effortless finesse I saw in my uncle's work. Although the wrestling match never evolved into dance, through the years I've grown to love the sport as an essential part of who I am.

With all this talk of drawing, isn't it odd that I never use it in my design work? To be more specific, I have almost never put pen to paper as a design solution. The pages in my notebooks are private records, a diary of sketches in preparation for some unrealized brilliance. As a public substitute, in recent years I've taken up collage as a contorted form of drawing. The lines themselves are preprinted. I slice them out of books and newspapers and twist them into a final form. The same with type. Each letter is cut from its original text and placed in my final tableau. An unusual kind of drawing made from an unusual kind of collage. With such tiny pieces, it's almost a mosaic. But instead of an overall plan, each new piece places itself in response to all the previous pieces. The accumulation shifts and changes slowly, like the marks in my notebook.

This meandering slowness is what I am after. I want each finished page to live on its own, with all the parts reacting to their own inner logic—the way that bugs crawl, trees grow, or rivers find their course. I see these paths as arguments, too. But they unfold without words, a billion visible conclusions derived from physical, conflicting forces. As dextrous or clumsy as they are, our hands are rooted in that natural world, along with ink and paper. There are limitations and properties that they can't ignore, but must tackle and resolve. The final work is a record of the struggle, and whether a mess or a masterpiece, it is brimming with life.

Our hands cannot keep away from the machine. This is the line I had planned as the start of my essay. I would have claimed that the machine acts as an extension of our body; that it replaces the organic, physical struggle with antiseptic mathematics. In many ways that relieves us of so much anxiety and I feel it as I punch the keyboard to form this text. That's how I would have gotten things started, but apparently I was wrong. What was to have been the beginning has turned into the conclusion. For my thoughts wander and slip, clouding over the clarity of my intentions. They refuse to walk a straight line, and I cannot write any better than I can draw a picture. That's to say, I can't seem to render these words into a proper external ideal. And that is why I can't write this essay.

04
GRAND FINALE

Garden flowers wrapped in brown paper,
love letters bundled with string.
The hand gathers and secures otherwise scattered notions,
infuses each printed page with a human presence
and the painstaking care of craft.
Whether a structural necessity or an
elegant embellishment, the finishing touch
of a sewn thread or a wrapped package transform
everyday communication into gifts.

Comment: The Independent Spirit Awards is the anti-Oscars. The ISAs toggle the line between a drunken party and a celebration of the independent film community—very casual, a little rowdy and sometimes unhinged. The graphics needed to bridge the fact that this was a daytime beach party in a bright white tent that would be aired on a channel that's bold, dark and essentially *punk*. In the spirit of the film industry and detached from Oscar-like formality, my approach was to play with the fashion and funky feeling of the ceremony while bringing the sunny, bright feeling of Santa Monica.

The Independent Spirit Awards

Design: Exopolis **Art Director:** Jorge Calleja
Designer: Jorge Calleja **Client:** IFC Channel
Materials: leaves, fabrics, sequins, boxes, sewing

UNLUCKY DAY DEC 31

SKYSCRAPER DAY FEB 3

MULTIPLE PERSONALITY DAY MAR 5

TWIN DAY AUG 4

PUNCH DAY SEP 20

NUDE DAY JUL 14

LOST SOCK DAY MAY 9

BLAME SOMEONE ELSE DAY APR 13

LAST MINUTE CHANGES DAY JUN 27

NO BEARD DAY OCT 18

PLAN YOUR EPITAPH DAY NOV 14

HUGGING DAY

TWIN DAY AUG 4

EVERYDAY IS A HOLID★Y

SEP05

S	M	T	W	T	F	S
				01	02	03
04	05	06	07	08	09	10
11	12	13	14	15	16	17
18	19	★	21	22	23	24
25	26	27	28	29	30	

designarmy.com

Everyday is a Holiday promotion

Design: Design Army **Art Directors:** Jake Lefebure, Pum Lefebure **Designers:** Dan Adler, Tim Madle **Illustrator:** Tim Madle **Client:** Design Army **Printer:** Admat, Graphik

Comment: The "Everyday is a Holiday" coaster-calendar is a set of twelve letterpressed coasters that are wrapped in a custom grommet shock-cord sleeve with a gift tag. As our holiday promo, we wanted to make sure our client had something to remember us by—every day! And yes, all of these holidays exist. We went through and picked out our favorites and then matched up fun illustrations for each one—a two-headed sheep for "Twin Day," a big hairy, masked wrestler for "Hugging Day," a peeled banana for "Nude Day," and our favorite—a three-legged rabbit for "Unlucky Day."

Sam and Josh promotional CD

Design: A Yellow Bird Machine **Designer:** Amy Martino **Client:** Sam and Josh **Materials:** canvas paper, sewing machine

Comment: I designed this CD label and packaging for a band that was sending their demo to agents and producers. The handmade quality went along with the grassroots way they were getting their music out there and felt more personal and memorable. You want your demo to be noticeable among all the other submissions. A needle in a haystack is impossible to find… but what if it were a needle printed on canvas paper and sewn into a pocket sleeve with a matching CD on the inside?

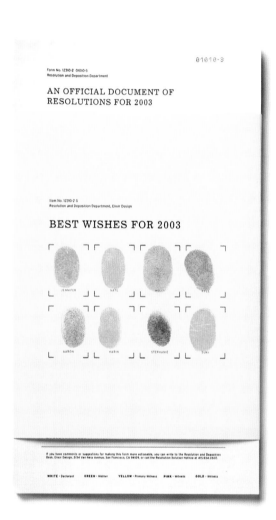

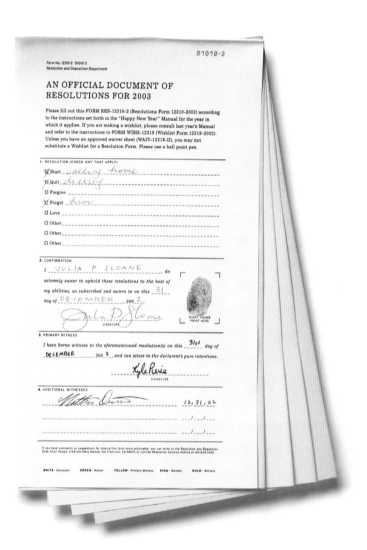

Elixir holiday card

Design: Elixir Design **Art Director:** Jennifer
Jerde **Designer:** Aaron Cruse **Copywriter:** Adrian
Lurssen **Client:** Elixir Design **Materials:** ink,
thumbprints **Printer:** Lauretta Printing

Comment: Fingerprints on this 2002 holiday promotion serve as signatures from each member of the studio, while providing an experience for its recipients: clients (past, current and future), family and friends. "An Official Document of Resolutions for 2003" was sent as a spoof from a governmental agency, and the fingerprinting, along with carbon copied forms, witness signatures and fabricated bureaucracy-speak, serve to heighten the effect. The project was economical, though time-consuming.

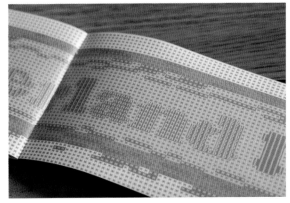

Luanne Martineau catalog

Design: Fishten **Art Directors:** Kelly Hartman, Giles Woodward **Designers:** Kelly Hartman, Giles Woodward **Client:** Medicine Hat Museum & Art Gallery **Materials:** knitted wool band, Mactac, board, paper, wire stitches

Comment: This exhibition catalog designed for artist Luanne Martineau would not be relevant or appropriate if it did not include a tactile component. The artist herself employs outmoded means of production to create hand-labor-intensive works. Our design supports this with a knitted wrap produced in the colorways used in the artist's knitted works.

Comment: The Bridge Fund promotes sustainable economic development, educational advancement, cultural preservation and environmental conservation on the Tibetan plateau. Inspired by Buddhism, the book initially appears to be a simple two-color text narrative, but once one tears the perforated signatures, it reveals beautiful four-color imagery of the people, places and results of The Bridge Fund's work. The annual was also conceptualized to support Tibetans directly by incorporating cover stock, logo printing and letter openers handcrafted by Tibetans.

The Bridge Fund annual report

Design: Volume, Inc. Art Directors: Adam Brodsley, Eric Heiman Designer: Adam Brodsley Client: The Bridge Fund Printer: Materials: handmade Tibetan paper, woodblock Printer: Dege Parkhang, Tibet (cover); Blanchette Press

Transfer acoustic show poster

Design: D5ive **Art Director:** Paul B. Drohan
Designer: Paul B. Drohan **Client:** Transfer Band
Materials: pencil, paper, copier, scanner, computer

Comment: This was a chance to do something completely different for Transfer, especially since they weren't playing at their usual bar-fly-infested joint. I wanted this poster to have a retro and more upscale look to it, mainly because University of San Diego is a Catholic college and it was going to be an acoustic, all-ages show. The photo is from Danny de La Cruz and the worn look was created by using scanned dirt and paper, plus some of my dirt brushes in Photoshop. The color palette is a reflection from the old jazz albums of the late 1950s.

0
9
4

FINGERPRINT

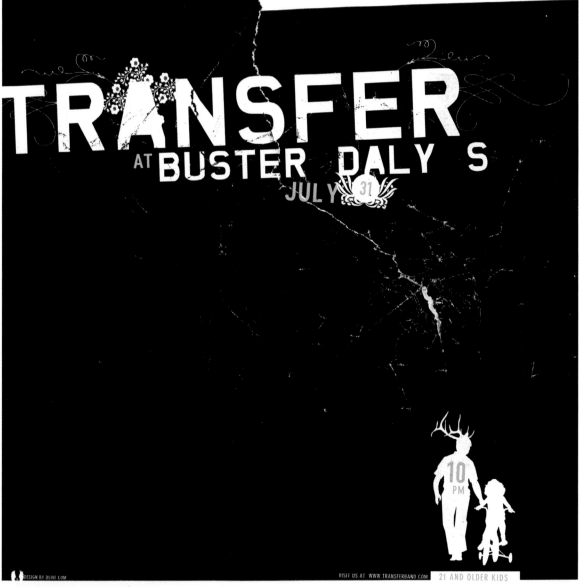

VISIT US AT WWW.TRANSFERBAND.COM 21 AND OLDER KIDS

Comment: This was the second poster I created for Transfer. We were still in the defining stages for them. I didn't know that much about the place they were playing, except that it was for people twenty-one years and older. I scanned a torn piece of paper, then laid the type out big. I wanted to use the flourishes to balance the rough feel of the poster. I thought the rip was cool to visually connect the top to the bottom and it sort of pointed to the guy with antlers and the kid. It's funny: everyone still loves that image of the guy and the kid.

Transfer at Buster Daly's poster

Design: D5ive **Art Director:** Paul B. Drohan **Designer:** Paul B. Drohan **Client:** Transfer Band **Materials:** pencil, paper, copier, scanner, computer

CHAPTER
04

Transfer at Ken Club poster

Design: D5ive **Art Director:** Paul B. Drohan
Designer: Paul B. Drohan **Client:** Transfer Band
Materials: pencil, paper, copier, scanner, computer

Comment: This poster had two purposes. One was to announce the band's gig and the other was to celebrate Jason Cardenas' (the guitar player's) thirtieth birthday. I wanted something that integrated an illustration I had done of him earlier. To represent the dual purpose of the poster, a split format was used. I photocopied some textures and handwriting for the background and used a font that David Carson designed for Nine Inch Nails. The font has a nice organic feel to it.

comment: When Tod Lippy rescheduled his visit to the School of Visual Arts at the last minute, I decided to modify the posters that had already been printed instead of reprinting the original design. Lippy is the man behind the arts magazine *Esopus*, which has a very textural feel and appeals to my love of paper. The background of the poster is a scan from the inside cover of a 19th century atlas that I picked up at a flea market; and to change the lecture date I affixed a library due date slip stamped with the new date. The rescheduling of this event was the best thing to happen to the poster's design.

Tod Lippy lecture poster

Design: School of Visual Arts **Art Director:** Amanda Spielman **Designer:** Amanda Spielman **Client:** School of Visual Arts **Materials:** library date due slip, date stamp **Dimensions:** 17 1/4" x 22 7/8" (45cm x 58cm)

STANDOUT PERFORMANCES DESERVE OUTSTANDING PACKAGING.

YESDESIGNGROUP
7220 BEVERLY BOULEVARD SUITE 202
LOS ANGELES, CALIFORNIA 90036

LORI J POSNER
YESDESIGNGROUP

LORI J POSNER
YESDESIGNGROUP
7220 BEVERLY BLVD SUITE 202
LOS ANGELES CALIFORNIA 90036
WWW.YESDESIGNGROUP.COM
T 323.330.9300 F 323.939.3911
LJP@YESDESIGNGROUP

YES DESIGN GROUP promotion

Design: YES DESIGN GROUP **Art Director:** Tim Gleason **Client:** YES DESIGN GROUP
Materials: comp board, cherry wood veneer

Comment: We feel this media kit represents our company as an innovator in the field of packaging. The handmade box that holds the printed pieces was conceived as a deconstruction of the interior. When opened, it is very polished-looking, complete with a foiled company logo on real wood veneer. The curves of the box and die-cut were carried through to the hand-applied exterior labels. We also shot images of our dimensional work on large cards that are tri-folded to fit into the casing.

SATUREIA HORTENSIS

CHRISTMAS *is a season that inspires us all to celebrate the joy of giving, of healing and of spreading the love as far as we can reach. This year we hope to send you our thoughts and gratitude as well as a humble token, for words are not enough to express the growing comfort of having you as part of our lives. Embedded in this card are seeds of sage. Upon reading, kindly save and lay on moist soil for planting.*

Have a memorable Christmas!

Randy and Barbara

SAGE is a hardy perennial, whose name is derived from Salveo, to save, and refers to the medicinal values the plants were thought to possess. Sage was one of the most valued herbs of antiquity. Not only is it a culinary herb, it is also used extensively in homeopathic remedies.

Salvation sustainable Christmas card

Design: Passing Notes, Inc. **Art Director:** Abbie Pianas Gong **Designer:** Abbie Pianas Gong **Client:** Randy & Barbara Powers **Materials:** letterpress, handmade paper, sage seeds **Printer:** Porridge Papers

Comment: During a season of celebration and giving—when much paper is accumulated and discarded—this card sends a sustainable message to its recipients. Created with specially milled papers embedded with sage seeds, the cards are intended to be saved and laid upon the soil for planting. The name "sage" is derived from *salveo* (to save), referring to the plant's medicinal qualities.

Modern Dog poster stamps

Design: Modern Dog Design Co. **Designers:**
Robynne Raye, Michael Strassburger, Clara Anders
Client: Modern Dog Design Co. **Materials:** sticky
back "postage" paper **Printer:** The Copy Company

Comment: We decided to put a bunch of our poster designs on a two-
stamp sheet, an idea that we've wanted to do for some time now. We printed
on gummed paper for authenticity. Then, putting the sheets in groups of
three, we sent them by hand through an old 1800s perfing machine. Each
page of stamps took seventeen passes through the old-school contraption,
and took around three to four minutes to complete.

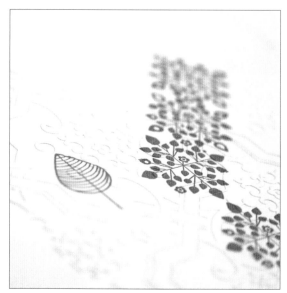

Office holiday card

Design: Office: Jason Schulte Design **Art Director:**
Jason Schulte **Designer:** Nicole Flores **Client:** Office:
Jason Schulte Design **Materials:** thread, letterpress,
hand-stamp, blind emboss **Printer:** Geertz Printing

Comment: We incorporated hand elements into Office's 2005
holiday card to make the experience for the recipient more special,
as if each is receiving a unique piece of art. The card evolved from
pages of hand sketches, and we tried to maintain this stream-of-
consciousness feel in the final execution. The techniques used in
creating the card included letterpress of hand-drawn art, blind
emboss, foil stamp and stitching to seal the glassine envelopes.

The word 'handmade' might not be the first to spring to mind
when you're sitting in a darkened theater watching the latest
blockbuster — awash with special effects, digitally generated
dinosaurs, giant lovelorn apes and actors striving mightily
to flee the inevitable fireball. If you do give any thought to
how the movie was made, you might get a mental image of
legions of geeks toiling over hot keyboards.

But that's only part of the story — a lot of the 'real'
stuff you see on the screen is custom designed and hand
produced. Sets, costumes and all kinds of props.
It constantly amazes me how many props — big and small —
are needed, even though I've been hired to provide many
of them for a few movies. Letters, legal documents,
land deeds, congressional acts, presidential seals, notebooks,
drawings, paintings, books of poetry and military tactics, quill
pens, ink bottles, wine labels, and ancient occult tomes —
all of it painstakingly researched and carefully crafted
by hand from scratch. Usually way too painstakingly and
carefully; I sometimes make minimum wage by the time
the smoke clears, but I wouldn't have it any other way.

Currently I work mainly as an illustrator, but my
background is in letterpress printing. I've spent days
setting and printing a single piece by hand, and I bring
that same compulsion to prop making. Did I really
need to hand typeset and hand print the hundreds
of labels, letterheads, fliers and voting ballots for
The Legend of Zorro? I would have made a lot
more money if I had just slapped something together
on the computer from faux old-timey fonts and

then simply photocopied it, and they would have been happy — I've seen some of the half-assed crap that prop houses sometimes get away with.

So why do I spend more time than I need to on these projects? Maybe its because it drives me crazy when I go to a movie and see the bad fake magazines and innappropriate digital fonts on 'period' documents. Maybe its because a movie feels so right when they take the time to get the details right. Or maybe because there's something incredibly satisfying about researching some obscure corner of design history and carefully replicating it. Or because I get to do something I love: I use my hands to work with real paper and ink and fire and knives and tools; hand set real metal and wood type; turn the crank of an old press. I love being surrounded by the smell of ink and oil and glue, the feel of good paper and leather, the sound the paper cutter makes as the blade slices through a stack of stitched book signatures. Or maybe I spend the extra time because I think people notice — maybe on some subliminal level — when the documents and writing instruments in a period movie are as carefully thought out as the costumes and sets. Perhaps the real reason is the thought that maybe, somewhere, one person is sitting in the dark, watching one of my props flash by on the screen, and for a split second they think, "Nice book!"

Ross MacDonald

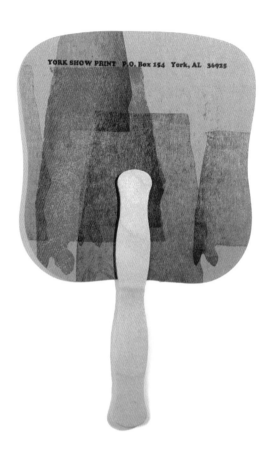

YORK SHOW PRINT P.O. Box 154 York, AL 36925

Buy Art fan

Design: Kennedy Prints **Art Director:** Amos Paul
Kennedy, Jr. **Designer:** Amos Paul Kennedy, Jr.
Client: Kentuck Festival of the Arts **Materials:**
chipboard, printed four colors **Printer:** Kennedy Prints

Comment: Kentuck Festival of the Arts is an annual arts and crafts show highlight-
ing work by southern artists. It is one of the largest art fairs in Alabama with more
than three hundred exhibitors and 30,000 visitors. For the last three years I have
been printing the posters for the art fair and the invitation to the patron party. In
2003, I printed these fans as gifts to the artists. I print stuff I think is cool and put
it out there for the world to see.

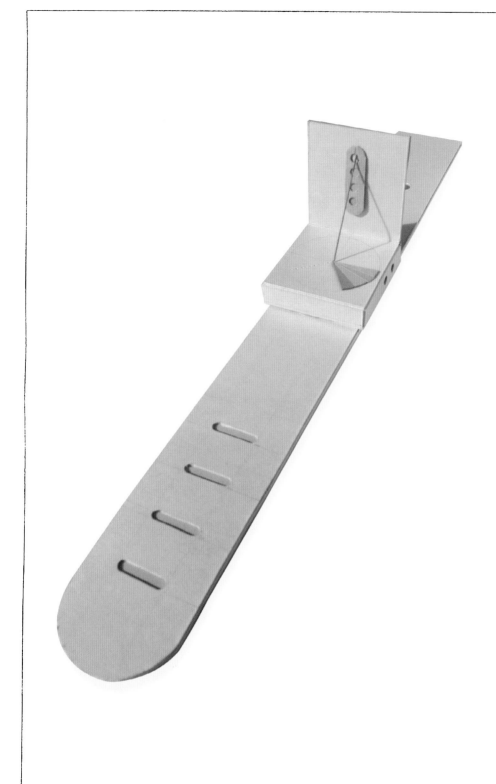

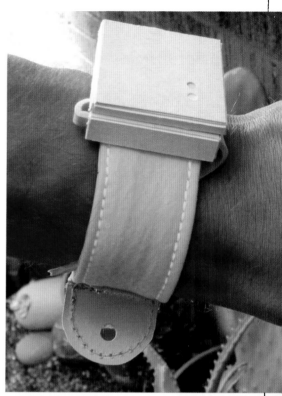

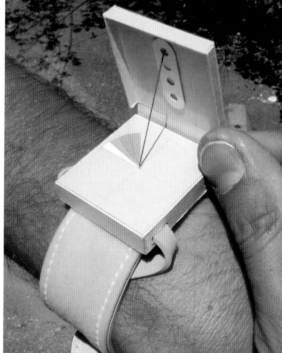

OBJET D'ART

Sundial watch

Design: Futurefarmers **Art Director:** Amy Franceschini **Designer:** Amy Franceschini **Client:** Orange County Museum **Materials:** paper, thread, fabric

Comment: The Sundial watch is a reaction to the ubiquity of technological devices in our lives today. It reminds us to depend on our own devices. It is an interface with nature: the sun will always rise in the morning and set in the evening, and the length of the winter days will be shorter than the summer days. This portable sundial physically illustrates the wonders of the sun and its motion through the sky providing a stage for the sun's shadow to dance. (Batteries not included.)

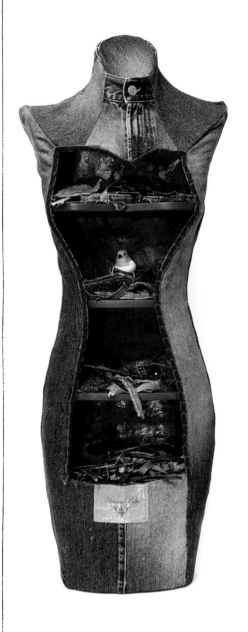

Avian Blue promotion

Design: Academy of Art University **Art Director:**
Thomas McNulty **Designer:** Sara Silva **Materials:**
mannequin, Diesel jeans, twigs, leaves, moss, old book
pages, velvet ribbon, iron-on transfer, paint, thread, staples

Comment: The Diesel jeans birdhouse was created as a promotion for
an imaginary new line of jeans dubbed "Avian Blue." A mannequin
evokes the provocative and sexy style of Diesel clothing; while the colors,
textures and Victorian elements convey the luxuriousness of the Avian
Blue line. Two pairs of Diesel jeans form the outer cover, the nests
are made out of foliage and strips of cut denim, and the interior is lined
with pages from old books about birds.

I Object book

Design: Simeon Man Kreative **Art Director:** Allan S. Manzano **Designer:** Allan S. Manzano **Client:** Simeon Man Kreative **Materials:** wood, nails, silkscreen, paper, Plexiglass, screws

Comment: The challenge: reinterpret an existing poster into a new, three-dimensional form that conveys emotion so deeply it evokes the viewer's own feeling. The poster depicts a series of nails portraying days confined in prison, a hammer and a mood that is more felt than seen. I thought it would be interesting to bring that emotion to life in a book format. The resulting design shows a form of escape. As the viewer turns, twists or digs through the pages, they begin to act out the idea of finding their freedom.

OBJET D'ART

TORTURE

THINK
AGAIN

NO DEATH
MURDER

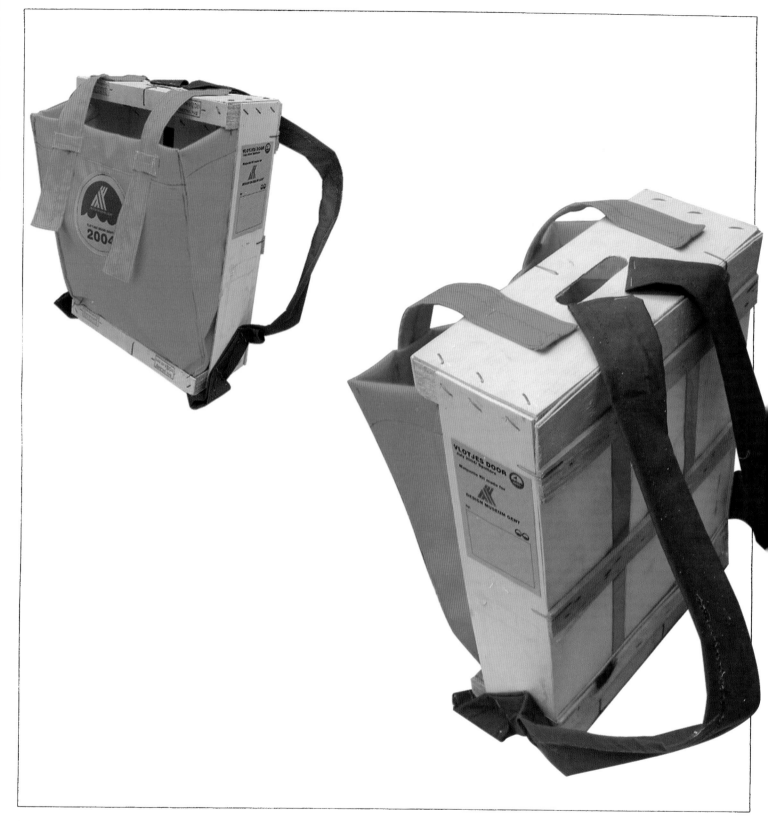

Fruit Box backpacks

Design: Futurefarmers **Art Director:** Amy Franceschini
Designer: Amy Franceschini **Client:** Spotters **Materials:**
found fruit boxes, canvas, thread

Comment: These backpacks were made for a children's workshop in Gent, Belgium. We used discarded fruit boxes to inspire the recycling of materials. The canvas was scrap material found at a local store.

The Sweetest Day invitation

Design: Passing Notes, Inc. **Art Director:** Abbie Pianas Gong **Designer:** Abbie Pianas Gong **Client:** Tom & Molly Denmark **Materials:** illustration, heating gun, embossing powder, paint **Printer:** Starshaped Press

Comment: Sweetest Day—celebrated on the third Saturday of October—is a reminder that a thoughtful deed gives life meaning. It was also the day on which Tom and Molly were wed. Invitations were graced with illustrations of the bride and groom's favorite sweets and encased in a glassine candy bag. A paintbrush on the spine of each booklet symbolizes how they met, their love for each other and the joy they share together as artists.

Edge book

Design: Lyonstreet Design **Art Director:** Emily McVarish **Designer:** Rachel Pedersen **Client:** Emily McVarish **Materials:** paper, photocopy machine, glue

Comment: Class: experimental type. Mental state: last semester in art school and burnt-out on looking at a computer screen. Project: Make a book using only definitions of the word "edge." Process: very little computer work, lots of paper and glue. The cover's sharp edges feel like falling off a cliff. I printed out definitions of the word *edge*, about one hundred times, all in Deepdene, a typeface with sharply pointed serifs, then created a story out of cut strips of the text. I wrapped type over the edge of the paper as well. The overall effect is visually strong, but what I feel is most powerful is its tactile quality.

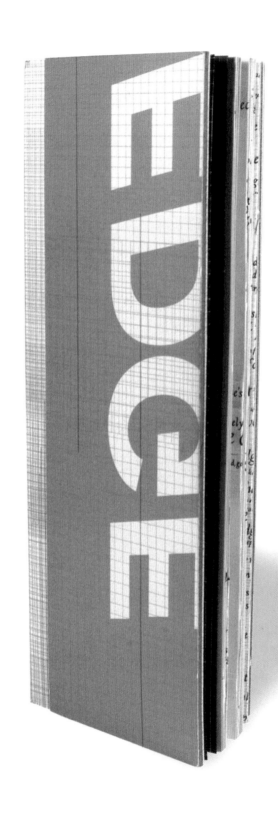

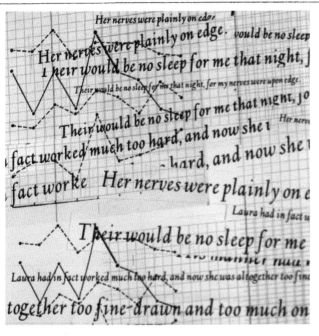

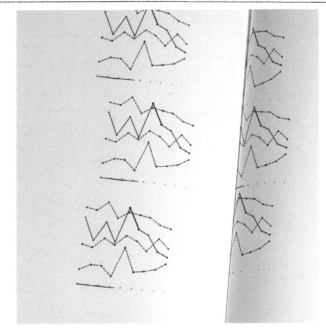

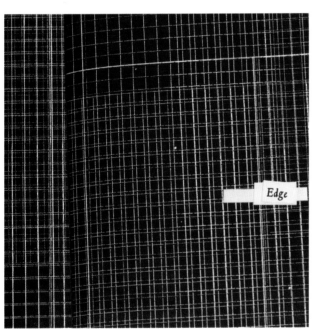

Design Madison posters

Creative Director: Dana Lytle **Designer:** David
Taylor **Illustrator:** David Taylor **Client:** Design
Madison **Materials:** birch boards, wood stain,
screen printing **Printer:** Planet Propaganda

Comment: Design Madison is a nonprofit organization with the goal to amplify the
impact that design plays in the structure of society and business. The audience for
all Design Madison pieces is designers. Designers are a hardened bunch, so getting
them to notice something usually takes an extra bit of thought and effort. On prior
"Speaker" posters, a simulated wood grain was used with the artwork to re-create the
feel of old wooden speakers. This series utilizes real birch boards from the lumberyard,
stained and then screenprinted by hand.

club (rĕd) direct mail postcard

Art Director: Bennett Holzworth **Client:**
AIGA Nebraska **Materials:** old book covers,
screenprinting, office address hand stamper
Printer: Bennett Holzworth, Adrian Hanft

Comment: To entice area designers to attend the AIGA's intimate graphic
design book club, I wanted this piece to be done almost entirely without
the computer. The covers are taken from old, unwanted *Reader's Digest*
condensed books. The front was screenprinted by hand, with lettering
based on antique letter stamps. The type on the back was painstakingly
stamped with a changeable four-line address stamper from Office Max.
These were successfully sent through the mail with a 60¢ postage stamp.

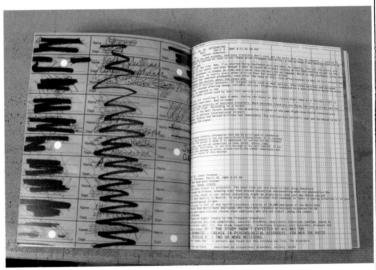

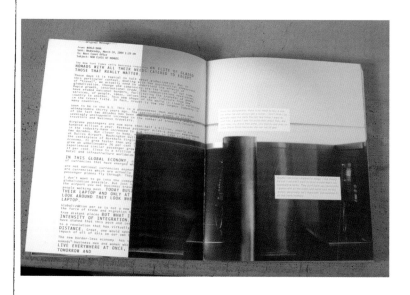

We work at home, in the car, walking down the street, just about everywhere. We are **A BOUNDARYLESS WORKFORCE.**

OBJET D'ART

Spent and Worked books

Design: Lyonstreet Design **Art Director:** Rachel Pedersen **Designer:** Rachel Pedersen **Client:** Lyon Street Design **Materials:** photos, type, graph paper, canvas **Printer:** BPS

Comment: These books seek to convey how unconnected we have become in an overly wired world. I was inspired to show it through the lens of my brother, who was constantly on the road for work. I wrote the story and took each photo that wasn't already in my parents' photo albums. The binding and simple insertions of French-folded, old-fashioned graph paper (on which e-mails to and from my brother were printed) make the craft and texture come alive, inviting and engaging the reader.

Design: Hammerpress **Designers:** Brady Vest, Lindsay Laricks **Client:** Stephanie Zerkel **Materials:** letterpress **Printer:** Hammerpress

Comment: This couple wanted a custom letterpressed wedding invitation that had both traditional and contemporary elements. They also didn't want it to feel overly feminine or masculine. This balance was achieved with a male-female collaboration at the studio. Brady designed a bold floral pattern for the sleeve and set the date of the wedding in big, chunky type on the band. Then Lindsay designed a delicate, feminine invitation inside using die-cut scalloped edges and dainty typography. By bringing the two different design styles together, we were able to give the couple exactly what they wanted.

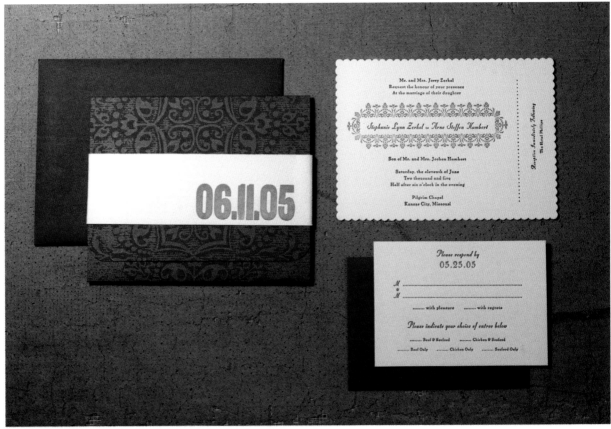

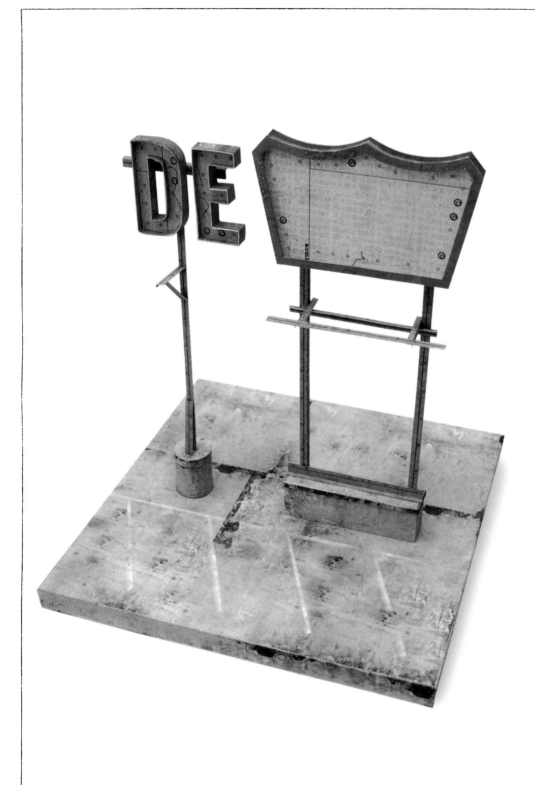

de{sign} paper construction

Design: Ahmann Kadlec Associates **Art Director:**
Geoff Ahmann **Designer:** Geoff Ahmann **Client:**
Ahmann Kadlec Associates **Materials:** digital outputs,
cut paper, foam core

Comment: de{sign} is a paper construction model about eight
inches tall—an iconic, typographic visual pun. It was created entirely
of paper and foam core. The textures were created in Photoshop, the
layouts in Illustrator, and output on Epson professional matte paper.
One acid-free all-purpose Elmer's glue stick and a small tube of Ace
no-run super glue gel supplied the adhesion. (I only super-glued my
finger to the foam core once.)

HOW I LOST MY VIRGINITY IN 2004 AT AGE 46

I work in a wooden world that first set type in 1879. Three years earlier, Alexander G. Bell had invented the telephone. Bell was aiming to change the future; the Hatch Brothers were simply looking for their first job. They became proprietors of Hatch Show Print, a letterpress job printer in Nashville, Tennessee.

One hundred twenty-seven years later, if one of the 25,000 visitors that visit Hatch annually makes it past the swinging gate and wanders back to my big wooden desk, they usually comment on my old rotary telephone. They say something like, "I haven't seen one of these in years." Eventually they get around to noticing the countless pieces of wooden type (although I wryly joke that we only have 26 letters at Hatch Show Print). Still, they seem to focus first on the telephone. Probably because it's the "antique version" of a tool they're familiar with, that they use every day.

I remember the first time I heard a customer's cell phone ring in the shop. "What's that new sound?" I thought. And when I saw this newfangled device I remember thinking, "More will be coming," like a Native American on the plains must have thought when he saw the first settlers rolling in. And arrive they both did. Now everyone on my staff—all of whom are in their twenties—has a cell phone. I don't have one and using one confuses me. (But I am proud to say I've learned how to book my own airplane tickets online.)

Just because something is invented doesn't mean you have to buy one and use it. At Hatch Show Print, it's more like "We have to use

it because it's here." We work in letterpress because letterpress is the shop's enduring technology, surviving every innovation in turn, whether silkscreen, offset printing, or now, electronic printing. I'm fond of saying that "the computer is the best thing that ever happened to Hatch." That sentence usually confuses the listener until I continue, "...because we're the antithesis of digital design." I was explaining this to songwriter John Prine the other day and he nodded in agreement saying, "Yeah, it draws a pretty clean line."

So here we are, in our third century of operation, creating posters for Coldplay that are drying next to B.B. King's run, leaning against the wall next to Willie Nelson's order, across the room from Pearl Jam, underneath Tim McGraw, leaning against Johnny Cash. He can hold 'em all up, the Man in Black (the color that only runs $6.50 a pound).

I'm still fascinated with the engineering that goes into each iron component of the printing press and the harmony of each gear working together to make words from letters as old as Hatch Show Print itself. I've always liked old things, and while I have an appreciation of new inventions, it's my job to keep most of them out of the shop. I can step easily in and out of the 19th and 21st centuries, slipping back and forth like a leaf through air, rising and falling in the sky with ink in my eye.

JIM SHERRADEN ★ HATCH SHOW PRINT
February 8, 2006

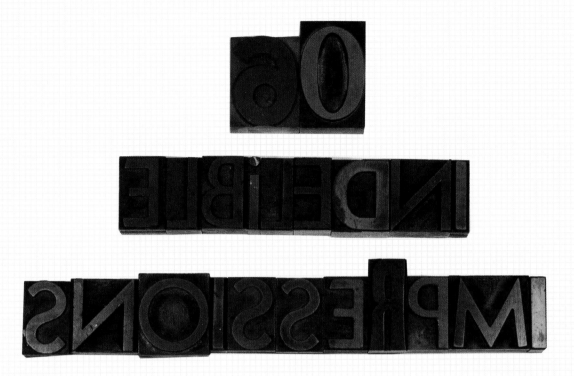

The physical exertion of setting the type,
cranking the press, wiping the ink,
or wetting the stamp are time-honored
rituals of creative production.
The rewards of sweat and time-intensive
labor are shown here;
the benefits of human investment over the machine.

AIGA unCoated, "the Crafty Issue"

 Designfarm, Anthony Dihle 12/28

Sew What poster

Comment: This limited-edition silkscreen print was produced for the AIGA DC chapter's quarterly journal, *unCoated*, and was featured in "The Crafty Issue," which focused on handmade objects. Anthony Dihle layered a variety of found patterns and design elements and used his craft of silkscreening—from pigment mixing to screen exposure and low-tech tools like a wooden squeegee and a soup spoon—to support the revived interest in the artist's hand and provide relief from a slicker, strictly computer-generated design.

Design: Designfarm **Designer:** Anthony Dihle
Client: AIGA Washington, DC **Dimensions:**
163⁄8" x 23" (42cm x 58cm)

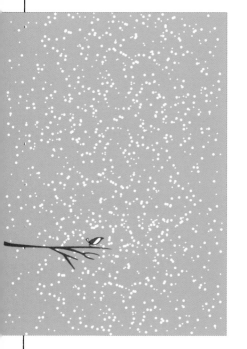

Templin Brink greeting cards

Design: Templin Brink Design **Art Directors:** Gaby Brink, Joel Templin **Designer:** Marius Gedgaudas **Client:** Templin Brink Design **Materials:** letterpress printed on blotter paper

Comment: Toward the end of every year, we try to make time to design a set of holiday cards. We use this project as an outlet for personal, creative expressions. These explorations often take us off the computer and into the realm of paper and scissors, a medium we don't use much in our client work, but one which perfectly conveys the warm and fuzzy nature of a holiday greeting.

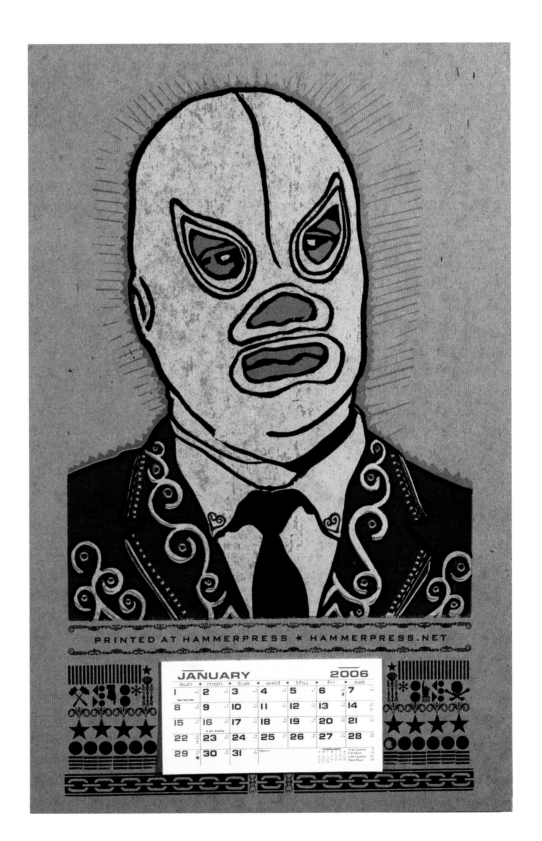

Comment: This 2006 calendar was produced using a five-color linoleum cut. The block was originally started for a wrestling benefit in Kansas City (don't ask) and then was set aside because it just didn't work. So we recycled it into a calendar. The image is actually a combination of a professional Mexican wrestler and Buck Owens—what Buck Owens would look like if he were a Mexican wrestler.

Fancy Wrestler calendar

Design: Hammerpress Designer: Matt McNary Client: Hammerpress Materials: letterpress, staples Printer: Hammerpress Dimensions: 11" x 17" (28cm x 43cm)

D15 poster

Design: Fuszion Collaborative **Designer:** John Foster
Client: Universidad De La Salle **Materials:** pencil, silkscreen inks, paper **Printer:** Standard Deluxe
Dimensions: 16" x 22" (41cm x 56cm)

Comment: I was incredibly honored by an invitation to speak at the "D15ENO" celebration for the graphic design program at the Universidad La Salle in Mexico City. I spoke about our firm's unusual client base in the DC area: in particular, the even split between national entertainment and packaging clients and our advocacy and philanthropic clients here at home. Using the title "I Can Eat With Both Hands," I quickly sketched what I wanted to convey in the promotional poster as well as my observations of current U.S. design trends. The final artwork was easily animated to accompany my presentation.

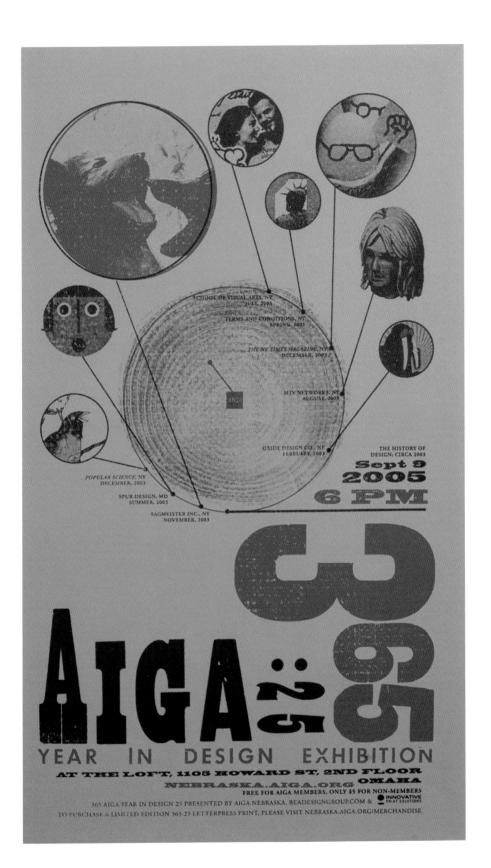

AIGA 365:25 event poster

Designers: Bennett Holzworth, Nate Voss **Client:** AIGA Nebraska **Materials:** letterpress wood and metal types, magnesium plate, tree stump **Printer:** Bennett Holzworth, Nate Voss **Dimensions:** 11" x 19"

Comment: This piece was entirely conceptualized and designed while the design world watched, on the blog Be A Design Group. While Nate Voss and I took turns making revisions, we decided to letterpress it as a limited-edition poster. To add another dimension, I wanted the process to be even more analog than the wood type and metal plates. We portrayed the year that the design selections represented by using an inked-up tree stump printed on the poster. This proved difficult, but we were eventually successful at running a piece of tree through an 85-year-old press.

Comment: To announce the AIGA's graphic design book club Christmas party, we created this poster for local design studios and colleges. While the design was created on the computer, the printing was done all by hand on a variety of wallpaper from the 1970s.

Art Director: Bennett Holzworth **Designer:** Adrian Hanft

Client: AIGA Nebraska **Materials:** 1970s wallpaper, screen-printing **Printer:** Adrian Hanft, Bennett Holzworth

Dimensions: 17¾" x 23¼" (45cm x 60 cm)

Comment: TJ Dovebelly has a very lush and experimental sound with a modern but strange Brazilian element. We wanted to make the packaging the opposite of what would be expected of a band that had a very electronic, almost hip-hop sound to it. The pattern came from a proof of actual lead ornaments that was digitally made into a large 14" x 22" magnesium plate. The original idea was to just use this plate, but we started playing around with blind embossing on press and then hand-rolling the ink over heavily impressed sheets of paper. After more experimentation and photocopy manipulation, the result was really unexpected. The object was transformed into this strange material that doesn't look at all like the cheap material it actually is.

TJ Dovebelly CD

Design: Hammerpress **Designers:**
Brady Vest, Katrina Schulze **Client:**
TJ Dovebelly **Materials:** letterpress
Printer: Hammerpress

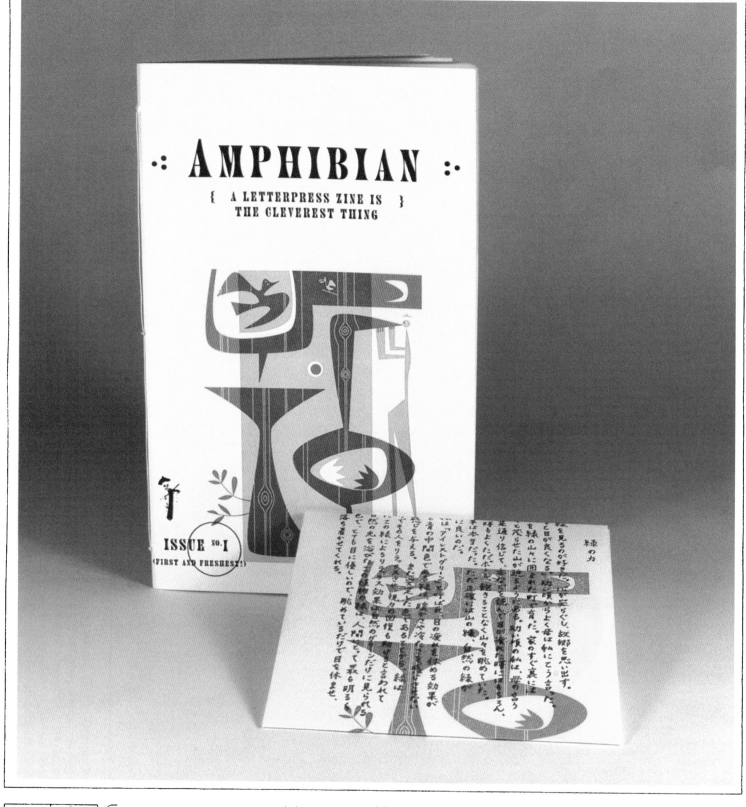

AMPHIBIAN zine

Art Director: Leif Fairfield
Designers: Various **Material:**
letterpress **Printer:** Leif Fairfield,
One Heart Press

Comment: *Amphibian*, a letterpress 'zine, seeks to combine the mystique and reverence attributed to fine letterpress printing with the gutter aesthetic and haphazard layout of an everyday homemade "zine." Most of the composition is done on press to preserve the distinct appearance of the issue being made by hand. Many hand-drawn illustrations and text are included in order to emphasize this point. The issue was designed to be an item that is at once personal and cherished, as well as something imperfect, and ultimately disposable. The 'zine passed though a Heidelberg Windmill press an estimated thirty to fifty times.

ISSUE I

THE **AMPHIBIAN**
LETTERPRESS ZINE
1039 Delaware Street
Berkeley Ca 94710

*LEMONS DO JUDO, EH?
DUST MAX.
ITTY TEA TOE GRAB NUTTY GUY.

$TATE MENT

k me when I tell them that I'm doing a letter
"So, what's th
labels, I like to be a bit elusive for the most
ne for years before you find out that I'm a v

BOAR
1947,1959,1971,198
stable and chivalrou

Pearl Jam Kitchener poster

Design: Ames Bros **Designer:** Coby Schultz
Client: Pearl Jam **Materials:** pen, ink, paint
splatter **Printer:** Seribellum

Office hand-drawn holiday card

Design: Office: Jason Schulte Design **Designer:** Jason Schulte **Client:** Office: Jason Schulte **Materials:** foil stamp, bookbinding material **Printer:** Geertz Printing

INDELIBLE IMPRESSIONS

Comment: The narrative reads, "Everyone assumed it was that unpleasant partridge from the pear tree. But it was Claire, the pigeon of peace." Our 2004 holiday card creates a fantasyland with hand-drawn flower flakes falling from the sky and a pigeon replacing the standard snow and partridge holiday motifs. Silver and white foil-stamping onto bookbinders' material was reminiscent of a holiday decoration that one of our designers created in second grade.

7 Brides for 7 Brothers poster

Design: Nordyke Design **Art Director:** John Nordyke
Designer: John Nordyke **Client:** Hartt School **Printer:**
John Nordyke **Dimensions:** 22¼" x 30" (53cm x 76cm)

Comment: Screenprinting was an economical means to provide large posters at low volume for this locally publicized production. *7 Brides for 7 Brothers* is a western romantic musical comedy. The genre and the ill-mannered brothers made appropriate a Western-inspired and crudely produced poster. The art and type were all drawn with a Sharpie and evidence of the marks are still evident in the tactile impression. By avoiding ink-jet or commercial printing, this solution fit the budget, publicity needs and communication needs of the performance.

FINGERPRINT

6 5 1

Comment: The Rachels is a group that plays beautifully lush and eerie chamber music. This poster is a mix of pre-existing plates we had made and artwork we chose specifically for this piece. The dark brown layer came from a book of cameos and silhouettes. When it was photocopied, it got stretched and did this weird funhouse-mirror-image thing that made it very mysterious. We then inverted the image and cut it as a negative plate and placed it on top of the previous layers. They liked the poster very much. We drank beer at the show and everyone was happy.

The Rachels poster

Design: Hammerpress **Designer:** Brady Vest
Client: The Rachels **Material:** letterpress
Printer: Hammerpress **Dimensions:** 13¼" x 24" (33cm x 61cm)

Red Antenna record

Design: Red Antenna **Designer:** Candy Chang **Client:** Red Antenna **Materials:** kraftboard, silkscreen

Comment: As a D.I.Y. record label, we produce smaller runs than the traditional label and wanted to celebrate this by providing our hand touch and stamp of approval on every single object. We created several stamps to use on our products, as well as our business cards and promotional materials. We used customized kraftboard sleeves with a die-cut edge as our canvas, and made as many of each record as we needed. For our next records, we explored more opportunity for individuality and silkscreened each cover with the artist's own design.

Office signed holiday cards

Design: Office: Jason Schulte Design **Designer:**
Jason Schulte **Client:** Office: Jason Schulte
Design **Materials:** letterpress, hand-stamp
Printer: Studio on Fire

Comment: Each 2002 Office holiday card was designed as if it were a
piece of art, signed by its respective holiday artist: Jean Gilbells, Lettit
Snoh and Frä Stee. We approached the design of the holiday card the
same way we typically approach art—by staying as close to the artist's
hand as possible. The hand-drawn letterpressed art lends a texture that
reinforced this idea.

Jean Gilbels

02

OFFICE jason schulte design 415 640 3660

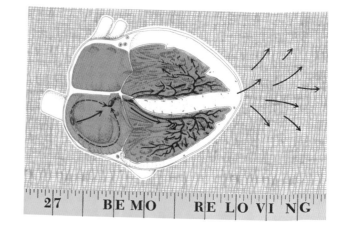

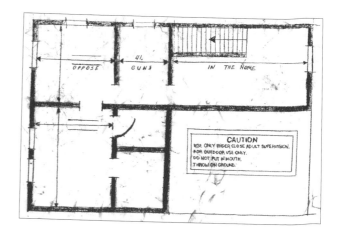

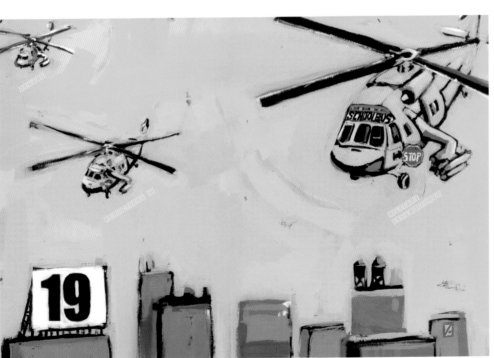

Comment: *Peace: 100 Ideas* redefines the traditional connotation of what constitutes an act of peace through the meaningful juxtaposition of ideas and imagery. Created by a collaborative team of designers and artists, the 100 innovative illustrations reveal and suggest further ways of thinking about and acting in support of peace. Hand-rendered elements in many of the illustrations convey a passionate immediacy and commitment that communicate at a very human level and strive to inspire further peaceful action.

Peace: 100 Ideas

Design: Chen Design Associates Art Directors: Joshua C. Chen, Max Spector Designer: Max Spector, Jennifer Tolo Pierce, Joshua C. Chen, Leon Yu, Gary Edward Blum, Brian Singer Client: CDA Press Materials: various Printer: Hemlock Printers

SF Ed Fund anniversary report

Design: Chen Design Associates **Art Director:** Joshua C. Chen **Designer:** Jennifer Tolo Pierce **Client:** San Francisco Education Fund **Materials:** pen, tracing paper, computer **Printer:** Oscar Printing Company

Comment: In celebration of its 25th anniversary, the San Francisco Education Fund requested a piece that would both commemorate the historic occasion and generate enthusiasm for future public involvement. A combination of archival and recent images of the children were paired with photography of the schools to underscore the progression from past to present to future. The hand-drawn lettering and charts provide a personal element that mirrors the children's drawings and conveys an energy that has distinguished the Ed Fund for over 25 years.

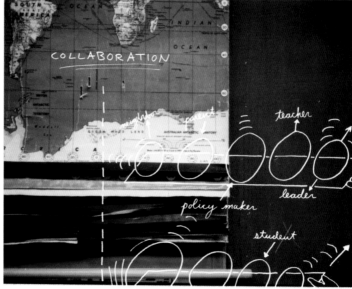

WINDOWS OF OPPORTUNITY
San Francisco Education Fund Programs

Throughout its twenty five year history, the Ed Fund has initiated programs with the intent of providing a direct link between the community and the schools, encouraging innovation in the classroom, and fostering supportive networks among both teachers and students.

While the end goal of all of our programs is to improve the quality of public education and to help our students meet necessary standards, the Ed Fund strongly believes that teachers are an invaluable and essential component in attaining this goal. We have supported the dedicated efforts of our city's teachers for twenty five years and strive to provide programs that will encourage dialogue and professional development among teachers, and richer curriculums and experiences in the classroom.

Collaboration is one of our primary values and a driving force in our relationships with the community and in our programs. Teachers and students not only develop beneficial relationships among themselves and with each other, they often establish strong links with the community. From visiting artists to experts in a particular field of study to free admission to a cultural institution, the Ed Fund programs bring the community into the schools and the schools into the community.

NETWORKS

The Ed Fund provides two programs — the Math and Science Network and the Literacy Network — that address the need for and benefits of supportive networks for teachers. Both programs are designed to bring teachers together to develop new and successful teaching strategies. In addition, these networks

14 San Francisco Education Fund

SAN FRANCISCO by Chen Design Associates

Definition: San Francisco

Design: Chen Design Associates **Art Director:**
Joshua C. Chen **Designer:** Jennifer Tolo Pierce
Client: AIGA SF **Materials:** watercolor, pencil,
pen, mixed media, Photoshop

Comment: AIGA San Francisco put out a call to designers to visually
define what San Francisco means to them. The selected entries became
part of an in-store installation at the Apple Store in San Francisco. This
entry utilizes painting and collage to celebrate the energy and eclectic
nature of the city and its inhabitants and to acknowledge the cultural
and natural richness that make the city such a compelling place to live.

MORE GREAT TITLES
FROM HOW BOOKS

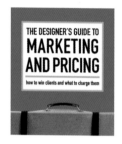

The Designer's Guide to Marketing and Pricing

This nuts and bolts guide to running a creative service business teaches you how to create a smart marketing plan—along with small actionable steps to take to reach financial goals. This book is the must-have guide for navigating the murky waters of the design business.

ILISE BENUM PELEG TOP

ISBN-13: 978-1-60061-008-0, ISBN-10: 1-60061-008-0, paperback, 256 p, #Z1042

IdeaSpotting / How to Find Your Next Great Idea

Seasoned business pro Sam Harrison offers real and unique insight into the creative process, as well as exercises to help anyone generate viable business ideas. *IdeaSpotting* trains business people to step outside of their daily routing to find their next great idea by encouraging spontaneity and exploration.

SAM HARRISON

ISBN-13: 978-1-58180-800-1, ISBN-10: 1-58180-800-3, paperback, 256 p, #33478

Rethink Redesign Reconstruct

This book is a powerful reminder that there's more than one solution to every problem—37 original projects followed by reinterpretations from top professionals serve as a creative jolt and inspiration for designers.

MARK WASSERMAN

ISBN-13: 978-1-58180-459-1, ISBN-10: 1-58180-459-8, hardcover, 192 p, #32716

These and other great HOW Books titles are available at your local bookstore or from online suppliers.

www.howdesign.com